LIVING GNOSTICISM

Living
Gnosticism

an ancient way of knowing

JORDAN STRATFORD
©MMVII

Apocryphile Press
1700 Shattuck Ave #81
Berkeley, CA 94709
www.apocryphile.org

Apocryphile Press Edition, 2007.
Copyright ©2007 by Jordan Stratford

Stratford, Jordan , 1966–
        Living Gnosticisme / by Jordan Stratford.
        ISBN 1-933993-53-7
        1. Gnosticism–Miscellanea
I. Title

Printed in the United States of America
Author photo: Davin Greenwell

AD REGINA AVIA

For the Lost Queen

ACKNOWLEDGEMENTS:

To my family – Zandra, Brendan, Liam, Xochitl, Sebastian, and Monica; to Bishop +Shaun McCann, Rev. Stu Berry, and Rev. Juliana Carnes of the Apostolic Johannite Church for their friendship and fraternity; to Bishop +Rosamonde Miller of the Ecclesia Gnostica Mysteriorum for inspiring me to become a priest and for her ongoing support; to Jeremy Puma of the Palm Tree Garden and Jesse Christopher Folks for their contribution to the "Four Point Plane" thematic definition of Gnosticism; to Rev. Terje Bergersen of the Ecclesia Gnostica for his longstanding friendship; to Reverend Mother Marsha Emerick+ of the Gnostic Church of Mary Magdalene for her friendship and vision for the Order of Saint Esclarmonde; and to my sister Avielah Barclay for her insight into Judaism and Kabala.

Scripture paraphrased from James M. Robinson, ed., *The Nag Hammadi Library*, revised edition. HarperCollins, San Francisco, 1990.

Illustrations are from details of various works by William Blake, 1757-1827

SURRENDER PRAYER

I have been apart and I have lost my way
The archons have taken my vision.
At times I am filled with Thee,
but often I am blind to Thy Presence
when all I see is this world of form.
My ignorance and blindness are all I have to offer
But these I give to Thee, holding back nothing
And in my hours of darkness
when I am not sure there even is a Thou, hearing
my call
I still call to Thee with all my heart.
Hear the cry of my voice, clamoring from this
desert,
for my soul is parched and my heart can barely
stand this longing.
       – +Rosamonde Miller

10

PREFACE

Most modern bookstores will offer a dozen or so works
on the Gnostics and their Gospels. Each of these texts
will leave you with the understanding that Gnosticism is
something odd that happened 1800 years ago or so, and that
the Gnostics now belong to the realm of historical curiosity
rather than religious experience. You are unlikely to
encounter the living, challenging tradition that is playing
out in the lives of thousands who will meet this weekend for
prayer, celebration, debate and community action.

You'll read elsewhere that Gnosticism is elitist, misogynist,
secretive, and world-hating. But the Gnostic scriptures
themselves speak of a philosophy that is universal; reveres
Eve as the first Saint and Sophia as a Goddess; is intimate
rather than occult; and finds Holy Wisdom under ever stone
and within every tree. You'll hear that Gnosticism is dualist,
claiming two equal and opposing gods; but Gnosticism has
always taught that we are all aspects of an infinite one-ness.

Most baffling of all, contemporary readers will be told that
the word "Gnosticism" is so vague and contradictory that it
never really existed – despite a rich continuum of seekers,
history, and scripture. Part of the challenge in studying
Gnosticism is that it has never been a monolith, never had
a canon of orthodoxy. It has always been less of a "set" and
more of an intersection of overlapping themes. The themes
themselves have an elusive, dreamlike quality that presents
many challenges for scholars used to tidy classifications.

Most of the confusion arises from identifying Gnosticism
with later, distinct movements: Marcionism and
Manichaeanism. While each of these borrowed from earlier
Gnostic ideas, they veered dramatically from Gnosticism's
original course – denying *gnosis*, the intimate understanding
of Divinity that is the core of Gnostic experience – and

therefore cannot be credibly regarded as part of Gnosticism at all. The distinctions are as sharp as Buddhism from Hinduism; as Christianity from Judaism. Worldly denial, radical dualism, and disregard for the Old Testament can be found in later movements, but not in Gnosticism *per se*.

Compare all these contradictions with the abiding reality of Gnosticism; an inclusive, participatory religious context that invites, inspires and nourishes. At the very center of Gnosticism is the enlightened moment of *gnosis*; an immediate, intimate and unique encounter with the Mystery and our place in it. Many schools of religious teaching in the West have rejected this transformative experience, due in part to the fact that it demolishes both Original Sin and the authority of scripture, setting in their place the Sacred Flame of our kinship with the eternal. Yet Gnosticism has never been extinguished, surviving in the shadows of orthodoxy, flowering throughout the centuries as myth and mysticism. Gnosticism prizes art over polemic, intuition over theology, curiosity over obedience.

Seeing this contemporary phenomenon, it's easy to categorize Gnosticism as "just another religion", with a core of religious texts, churches, clergy, rites for certain days of the year – and in a very real sense that's true. But Gnosticism is also a way of seeing; a technique for working with a set of tools that begin with a specific myth; but it does not end there. Gnosticism is ultimately pragmatic, adapting to the spiritual experience and imaginative daring of each explorer. While this book illustrates a picture of contemporary "organized" Gnosticism, most Gnostics are solitary *confreres*, contemplating and creating in coffee shops and living rooms. While Gnosticism can express itself via a tradition of incense and candles and sacraments, it is equally expressed in art galleries, in charity, in social action – and in discrete moments of liberating clarity.

There is in everyone the divine power existing in a latent condition... This is one power divided above and below; generating itself, making itself grow, seeking itself, finding itself, daughter of itself, son of itself – mother, father, unity, being a source of the entire circle of existence.

> – *The Great Announcement*,
> quoted by Hippolytus c. 200 CE

13

14

I. KNOW THYSELF

It seems to me that the only true Christians were (are?) the Gnostics, who believe in self-knowledge, i.e., becoming Christ themselves, reaching the Christ within. The Light is the Truth. All any of us are trying to do is precisely that: Turn on the Light.
– John Lennon,
The Mysterious Smell of Roses

Twilight. A group of figures, some robed in traditional white albs, most in plain clothes, pace the ancient patterns of the labyrinth in wet grass and silent meditation. Later, inside a small chapel rented from a larger church, yellow, red, blue and green candles are lit and prayers are offered, invoking the four elements and their associated Archangels, and lastly a white candle in a silver orb. The rite begins with a Greek chant associated with the Temple at Delphi. *Logos* and *Sophia*, Word and Wisdom are invited to the *Heiros Gamos*, the Sacred Marriage. The priest intones:

> *"Come, hidden Mother, come; come, you who are made manifest in your works, and give joy and rest to those who are bound to you. Come and partake in this Eucharist which we perform in your name, and the agape for which we have assembled at your invitation."*

The words are at least 2,000 years old from Gospels considered too heretical for other faiths. Later still a chalice of wine is blessed and shared among those gathered, offered with the benediction:

> *"Be what you see; receive what you are."*

The rite is startling in its simplicity and solemnity. One imagines a medieval chapel having a similar tone. Worship is careful, poignant and almost nostalgic.

Those assembled understand themselves to be a kind of royal family in exile; castaway Sparks of God, homesick for union, imperiled by a spiritual amnesia. These are the Gnostics, holding in their imagination symbols and ideas persecuted for centuries. They employ myth and dreams and poetry as practical tools in their reunion with the Divine.

In a very real sense, they are the Secret Church of the Holy Grail.

Gnosis means "knowledge"; a specific kind of intimate knowledge, the way lovers know one another. The root of *gnosis* hides in the more familiar words *recognize, cunning,* and *narrative.* For spiritual seekers, *gnosis* is deep understanding of the Divine and our relationship to it. Dutch scholar Gilles Quispel explained it as "knowledge of the heart"; quite simply, *gnosis* is enlightenment.

> This *gnosis* is not something that can be put into words like other sciences; but after long-continued conversation between teacher and pupil, in joint pursuit of the subject, suddenly, like light flashing forth when a fire is kindled, it is born in the soul and straightaway nourishes itself.
> – Plato, *Seventh Letter*

Gnosticism is a pre-Christian religious tradition that fuses Judaism, Greek philosophy and the Mystery Schools of the ancient world. Originating in the intellectual "café societies" of Alexandria around 200 BCE, the original Gnostics were

Greek-educated Jews, living in Egypt, on the doorstep of the Roman Empire. Theirs was the realm of diverse and interplaying cultures, of ideas and imagination. Gnostics unflinchingly explored the borders of myth and archetype, of metaphors and dreams, of creativity and poetic expression.

While it does seem odd to found a religion in an ancient Egyptian Starbucks with a group of Jews debating Greek philosophy, this is precisely where our story begins: in the Paris-in-the-20's of the ancient world, with artists and initiates inhaling the erotic perfume of dangerous ideas.

They were wrestling with the issues of the origins of good and evil, of human nature, of the role of God and wisdom in the world, of the seeming conflict between Grace and free will. The tools with which they addressed these ideas were natural curiosity, the Jewish value of literacy along with ancient Semitic magics, Plato and Aristotle, and the ambient, connecting mysticism out of which their entire culture was based. Their discussions resulted in texts such as *The Book of Enoch* and *The Book of Sophia* around 160 BCE, and the *Corpus Hermeticum* some 200 years later.

Thousands of years later, Beat poet Allen Ginsberg would write a fitting description of these inspired, impassioned myth-makers;

> angelheaded hipsters burning for the ancient heavenly connection to the starry dynamo in the machinery of night
> – *Howl*, 1955

Early Gnostic texts are identified by four principal characteristics:

> - that it is *gnosis*, not faith, that saves us from deception ("Gnostic Soteriology");
>
> - that the universe "flows out of" God, the way ripples emanate from a stone dropped in water ("Emanations Cosmogeny");
>
> - that the "Spark" of Divinity is immediately present in the world and constantly available to us, even if it is obscured by illusion and ignorance ("Immanent Pneumatology"); and
>
> - that this Spark's origin in the Infinite is revered by sacramental Mysteries, such as baptism and the eucharist ("Sacramental Theology").

Contemporary Gnostics would add a further point; that the system or daily world of our experience – one of deadlines, "spun" media, spilled coffee, parking tickets, and traffic jams – is an artificial construct, and we have a responsibility to wake up from this illusion into a real, spiritual world outside of "the powers that be". Modern Gnosticism tends to focus on this idea of "false reality" versus "waking up".

> The Matrix cannot tell you who you are.
> –*The Matrix*, 1999

Gnosticism amplifies and celebrates this "waking up", yet it is not a "path" to enlightenment. So Gnosticism does not lead to *gnosis*, but instead it was *gnosis* that lead these ancient beatniks to invent the myths and symbols of the Gnostic religion, to deepen it and enable it to shape their lives.

The central message of Gnosticism is "Know Thyself"; and while this phrase makes most people think of self-help seminars and ego-worship, it's actually quite different. In the Gnostic story, we are all lost fragments of God, and to "know yourself" is to recognize the serene dignity and immense responsibility of this heritage.

> Do not be ignorant of me.
> For I am the first and the last.
> I am the honored one and the scorned one.
> I am the whore and the holy one.
> – *The Thunder: Perfect Mind*

Gnosticism was tremendously influential in early Christian communities. Gnostic myths were re-interpreted to include characters of the Christian story: Jesus and Mary Magdalene, Philip, Thomas, James, Judas. The fluid, innovative style of the Gnostics adapted easily to the new religion, recognizing in it the eternal themes of incarnation, sacrifice and resurrection known to the Mystery Schools for thousands of years. Where a later mainstream Christianity worshipped Christ as a unique "event", Gnostic Christians pursued their spiritual liberation by becoming Christ-like. They exalted Mary Magdalene as an Apostle, saw Judas as an initiate of secret teachings, and viewed the serpent of the Garden of Eden as a liberating heroine.

Among these Gnostic Christian texts is the *Secret Book of John*, taken by some early Christian communities to be the sequel to the *Gospel of John*, and the original teachings of John the Baptist. It details a challenging myth of the origin of the world, of the role of Wisdom, of the creation of humanity, and of our liberation by *gnosis*.

Throughout centuries, Gnosticism survived as a subculture within Christianity, every so often appearing as heretical movements such as the Cathars, against whom a merciless crusade was called by Rome. Catharism was ultimately the result of a Gnostic take on the writings of St. Paul; that we are spiritual beings from a spiritual realm, temporarily placed in a world of cruelty and warfare.

Like Tolkien's Elves fighting "the long defeat", the Cathars passed inevitably from a world in which they were strangers – a world for which they held a detached but reverent stewardship – to their true home on a distant shore. A century of mass burnings, tortured confession, and the massacre of over 100,000 civilians turned neighbour against neighbour before the Inquisition, and Catharism was reduced from the flower of medieval civilization to the ashes of history.

Gnosticism also shaped the birth of Islam, the mystery cult of the Knights Templar, the Renaissance humanists and Alchemists. Gnosticism is the underground stream of Western religion, a current of recurring archetypes of myth and mysticism.

> "And she began to speak with the words of Life, and she remained in the presence of the Exalted One, possessing that which she had received before the world came into being.
>
> – *The Thought of Norea*

Despite Christianity's later rejection of Gnostic influence, the two religions are like strands in a braid – seemingly moving in opposite directions, yet serving to strengthen and inform one another. Gnosticism reveres many Christian Saints including Mary Magdalene, Hildegard von Bingen, Francis of Assisi, John of the Cross and Joan of Arc. Also here are other visionaries; Giordano Bruno, Julian of Norwich, William Blake. On the "outside", Gnosticism seems very Catholic in liturgy and organization; on the "inside", however, Gnosticism has profound similarities to Buddhism, both ethically and philosophically. The emphasis is on personal responsibility for spiritual work, contemplation, and mental discipline.

In *"The Allure of Gnosticism"* Edward Conze details these similarities between Gnosticism and Mahayana Buddhism; defined stages of spiritual development, the presentation of Wisdom as feminine, the priority of participatory myth over historical fact, the emphasis on re-union with the infinite One, and the distinction between an "organizer god" and the infinite godhead. There are also numerous comparisons to be made between the tradition of Vajrayana Buddhism and the later Hermetic texts.

Through the long millennia, Gnosticism remained in the Christian shadow, eventually to be declared extinct by religious scholars. But a Victorian interest in oriental mysticism such as Buddhism and Zoroastrianism renewed study of Gnostic scripture. The story of Gnosticism was found not in Eastern idols but in the blackened stones of Provençal castles, in the familiar stories of King Arthur and the Holy Grail, and ultimately in the very heart of Western religion itself.

As modernism dismissed the superstitions of a pre-Enlightenment era, Gnosticism was a spiritual absinthe for the counter-culture of artists, writers and freethinkers of the late 19th century. Through the romantic narratives of the Pre-Raphaelites to the sinuous vines of Art Nouveau, the esoteric language of the West was redeemed and celebrated. Tapestries of Grail maidens, Greek Goddesses and seasonal dryads provided the backdrop for the Gnostic Restoration which was to unfold.

The 1800s had sent the shockwave of the industrial revolution throughout the world, with the advent of automatic weaponry, the world-shaping power of the railway, the telegraph, microbiology and immunology, electricity, and refrigeration. These dramatic changes also had an impact on the religious landscape; resulting in the emergence of movements like Mormonism, Christian Science, and Theosophy. A new technological reality demanded a new psychological reality, and the questioning of the status quo gave birth to not only Marx and Freud, but also in reaction created an opportunity for the sleeping archetype of the Divine Feminine to return to full flower. Mucha's maidens marched gracefully to the forefront of the Western imagination.

In 1889, a French cleric named Jules Doinel received a vision of Sophia, the Goddess of Wisdom. She instructed him to revive the Gnostic Church of the Cathars, and described Wisdom's exile from the "Fullness" (*Pleroma*). She warned against the "half-creator" (*Demiurge*) of the false, everyday world, and told him to receive the Holy Spirit. In September of the following year, Doinel heeded his vision and founded the Gnostic Church in France, declaring 1890 "the year of the Gnosis restored".

Doinel was unknowingly following in the footsteps of another Frenchman, Raymond Fabré-Palaprat, who in 1804 had re-established the Gnostic "Johannite" church of John the Baptist and the first Christians. The Johannites immersed themselves in the symbolism of the Templars, as well as the treacherous court politics of the Napoleonic era. Interestingly, there is an unbroken Gnostic lineage which stretches back to community of John the Baptist: the Mandaeans of Iraq, dispersed now by civil war, who number perhaps some 70,000 in a worldwide diaspora. Other surviving ancient Gnostic offshoots include the Druze of Israel and the Yezidis of northern Iraq.

Through the 1890s, Doinel's Restoration attracted numerous Freemasons, Theosophists, Spiritualists, artists and poets, until Doinel suffered a crisis and left the Church to return to his Roman Catholic roots. The Gnostic Church expanded, struggled with scandal and schism, eventually "finding its feet" and sending branches throughout Europe, and in 1900 Doinel re-converted to Gnosticism.

> Light and Darkness, life and death, right and left, are brothers of one another. They are inseparable. Because of this neither are the good good, nor evil evil, nor is life life, nor death death. For this reason each one will dissolve into its earliest origin. But those who are exalted above the world are indissoluble, eternal.
>
> – *The Gospel of Philip*

In 1913, an ordained bishop in the apostolic ("Old Dutch Catholic") tradition consecrated a number of Gnostic bishops, now rendering their sacraments as "valid yet illicit" in the eyes of Rome, a validity bestowed to the earlier Johannites by Bishop Mauviel. This gave Gnosticism a legitimacy in a day and age where the sacraments were not seen as symbolic but as actual, miraculous events.

Renowned psychologist Carl Jung placed Gnostic myth and symbolism at the center of his work, and in 1916 produced a Gnostic prose-poem entitled *The Seven Sermons to the Dead*, using the *nom de plume* of Basilides, a second century Gnostic teacher:

> The Dead came back from Jerusalem, where they found not what they sought. They prayed me let them in and besought my word, and thus I began my teaching.
>
> Harken: I begin with nothingness. Nothingness is the same as fullness. In infinity full is no better than empty.

> Nothingness is both empty and full. As well might ye say anything else of nothingness, as for instance, white is it, or black, or again, it is not, or it is. A thing that is infinite and eternal hath no qualities, since it hath all qualities.

> This nothingness or fullness we name the Pleroma. [...] The dead now raised a great riot, for they were Christians.

Jung's friend Hermann Hesse published the Gnostic novel *Demian* in 1919. Invoking the Gnostic character known as *Abraxas*, the book is disguised as a "coming of age" story, a retelling of the ancient myth of the hero slowly identifying himself with his higher, enlightened Self .

As a resurrected Gnosticism grew in popularity among the writers and thinkers of the early twentieth century, it also attracted the attention of repressive governments and invading armies: The Gnostic bishop Constant Chevillon was martyred by the Gestapo in 1944 for working with French Resistance forces.

1945 brought forth a gift from the Egyptian desert: an earthen jar containing a treasury of ancient Gnostic scriptures now known as the Nag Hammadi Library. Revealed were entire Gospels only hinted at by history; sweeping poems of which only scraps had been known, and for the first time in over fifteen hundred years, Gnosticism spoke with its own voice.

> I am the light that is over all things. I am all: from me all came forth, and to me all attained.
> Split a piece of wood; I am there.
> Lift up the stone, and you will find me there.
> – *Gospel of Thomas*

Today these scriptures are woven through liturgies attended by thousands of Gnostics throughout the world. Far removed from the big-screen-TV services of megachurches, and even from the guitar Masses and tie-dyed vestments of modern Catholic ritual, Gnostic celebrations retain a solemnity and quiet dignity that has always been fundamental to Wisdom's invitation. Gnostics are called to the Sacred Marriage of Sophia, who is also the *Shekhina* or Presence of God, and the *Logos*, the Living Word: together a powerful message of balance and inclusion.

> What else is death except ignorance? What else is darkness except forgetfulness? Cast your anxiety upon God alone. Do not become desirous of gold and silver, which are profitless, but clothe yourself with Sophia like a robe; put *gnosis* on yourself like a crown, and be seated upon a throne of perception. For these are yours, and you will receive them again.
>
> – Silvanus, second century Gnostic teacher

25

Why then, the recent attention to such a small religious movement? Santeria practitioners, Rastafarians and even members of the "Jedi Religion" outnumber Gnostics by the millions, yet these groups attracts a fraction of media exposure given to Gnosticism. This is all the more remarkable for Gnosticism's lack of spectacle.

Before becoming Pope Benedict XVI, Joseph Ratzinger suggested Gnosticism was the single greatest threat to orthodox Christianity. Mainstream bookstores will offer a dozen books on the Gnostic *Gospel of Thomas* and of *Gospel of Mary Magdalene*, or on Sophia in her role as the Divine Feminine. Gnostic scripture shows up in television commercials for perfume. Major news magazines routinely cover advances in archaeology and discoveries of new Gnostic texts, such as the *Gospel of Judas*.

Gnostic works permeate popular culture, in films such as *The Matrix, Pan's Labyrinth, The Golden Compass,* and *V for Vendetta*; in the many novels of Philip K Dick; in the graphic novel *Promethea* and the music of Tori Amos, Joni Mitchell and David Bowie. These works deal with themes of identity, memory, liberation from a false reality, the value of beauty and the reconciliation of paradox, while deliberately employing Gnostic figures and terminology.

I think that this exposure is due to the fact that *gnosis* is occurring to us in flashes all the time, and that our materialist, scientific worldview is as incapable of finding a place for it as is mainstream religion. Millions are having mystical experiences with no familiar reference for these in churches which allow for only faith. Confronted by unacceptable dogma on one hand, and ministries carved out of solid blocks of marketing surveys on the other, people are hungry for the immediacy and intimacy of Wisdom. They are starving for *gnosis*.

> Hearken to the Logos, understand *gnosis*, love life.
> – *Secret Book of James*

So what is it that Gnostics "Know"?

The principle of Gnosticism – "Know Thyself" – resides at the core of any Seeker's journey: *"Who am I? Why am I here?"*

Gnosticism answers that *who you are* is a fragment of God, and co-existent with eternity. You were not created with your body, but you have always existed as part of the Fullness. The *why* of things is described as *theosis*, or becoming God, which is really just a kind of remembering

that, together, we are *already* God. To re-member, to
forget our forgetting and re-unite with the Fullness – what
the *Gospel of Philip* refers to as the Mystery of the Bridal
Chamber.

This knowing is not secret or occult knowledge, like a magic
word, but it is deeply personal. I can't tell you the answer
to your own "know thyself" equation any more than you can
tell me mine. We're not used to seeing spiritual information
in this way; personal as opposed to universal. The purpose
of Gnostic myth is not to declare "this is what happened and
it's true for everybody". It invites, suggests, asks, wonders.

Your union with the Divine is an unique process; an
intensely intimate and sacred space within. On hearing of a
Gnostic's mystical experience – as described in *Dark Night of
the Soul* or the poetry of St. Hildegard – many who have not
had this experience can be dismissive; but just as many are
inspired to ask deeper questions, to venture further along
their own path.

Tradition holds that path leads to the Chapel Perilous; an
interval of reflection and resistance that is often frustrating
and discouraging. Like the Hanged Man of the Tarot or
Christ on the Cross, there is a period of suspension, of
submission, of powerlessness while the transformation takes
place. It is only the instinctive hunger for reunion which
propels the Seeker forward, to go beyond the comfort of
routine and experience to quest for the Grail; to remember a
wholeness that existed before this journey, this exile.

The Hymn of the Pearl is a Gnostic myth of a Prince, sent
from a Kingdom in the East (Heaven) westward into Egypt
(the material world) on a mission for his Father, the King.
Upon arriving in Egypt, he eats the food (engages with the
"system") and falls into a deep sleep (*amnesis*), forgetting his
heritage and mission. He is lost, confused, and blinded to
his spiritual reality – as are we all.

In the story, a secret message is smuggled to the Prince. Upon receiving it, he remembers who he truly is, defeats a Dragon and returns a precious pearl (his own spark of Divinity) to the Kingdom. This is the letter he receives:

> From thy Father, the King of Kings,
> and thy Mother, the Mistress of the East,
> and from thy Brother, our second in Authority,
> to thee our Son, who art in Egypt, greeting!
>
> Call to mind that thou art a Son of Kings!
> See the slavery, – whom thou servest.
> Remember the Pearl,
> for which thou was sent to Egypt!
>
> Think of thy robe,
> and remember thy splendid toga,
> which thou shalt wear and with which thou shalt be
> adorned, when thy name hath been read out in the
> list of the valiant, and thy brother, our viceroy,
> thou shalt be in our kingdom.

You are the Prince in this story. The moment of *gnosis* is the reception of such a letter: the remembering of who you are and where you come from; that you are of the same stuff of the Father, of Sophia who is Holy Wisdom, of Christ who is your Brother. So where is your letter? What is the signal being sent to you right now to remind you of who you truly are?

Such things are the root of all good stories – you're not really a farm boy from Smallville, you're a super-powered alien from another world; you're not just Harry who lives under the stairs, you are the magical hero of important and dramatic events — but your real identity has been hidden from you by ignorant and limiting forces. This story never goes away, because in a very real sense it's true, and always has been.

We get signals constantly from the Mystery which is right in front of us, but there's also a very specific set of forces intent – willfully intent – on jamming those signals. Therefore a kind of negotiation emerges whereby the signals are encoded, and it time decoded by those committed to listening, to receiving. Being a Gnostic is like being a secret agent for God: Imagine members of the Resistance listening to a crystal radio in the cellar, deciphering transmissions; *"The woodpecker flies at midnight."* The signals are very specific, very personal, but their interpretation and incorporation is vital. This is the work of the Gnostic.

We have these signals before us; psychology, scripture, history, experience. And we have tools with which to decipher the signal; our creativity, our intellect, our compassion, wit and intuition. It's not surprising then that our understanding of that signal evolves over time, that we're changing the landscape by walking through it. This is why it's important for us not to try to be thirteenth century Cathars or second century BCE Alexandrians, but citizens of the 21st century, using the gifts of unique perspective and our courage to negotiate with the forces shaping the world today. The burden of such personal responsibility, and the sense of "the long defeat" are tempered by the sheer, blinding beauty of it; the intimate and undeniable knowledge of who are, of where we come from.

THE GNOSTIC CREED

What makes us free is the *gnosis*
of who we were,
of what we have become;
of where we were,
of wherein we have been cast;
of whereto we speed,
of wherefrom we are redeemed;
of what birth truly is,
and of what rebirth truly is.

> – *Excerpta ex Theodoto*

ANTHEM OF THE EXILED PRINCES

We are the Gnostics. We are exiled Princes, all of us; and in our exile we taste sorrow, and hope, and a secret prayer. Before a darkness greater than what we are, yet less than what we were, we tremble but do not cower. We grieve, but we do not despair.

We are the Knights of the Lost Queen, Companions to the Beloved: She of red egg and alabaster jar. The Alchemists and Kabalists, the Witches and Magicians are of us. We are the keepers of a Flame far older than the world, and we seek it out where we may find it, and breathe it to life with our wit, our humility, our art and our joy.

We stood before the murderers of Hypatia, and again before the fires of Montsegur, even as our blood stained both smoke and snow. Our history is forbidden, our language contraband. Our knowing sleeps beneath our anonymous skin.

We are the heirs of the Temples of Kemet, of the Mysteries of Helenic vineyards, of the River. Those who Quest are of us, whether armed with sword and chain in service to the Graal, or by alembic and crucible in the unveiling of Wisdom's Stone. We are all that stands against the returning of gold into lead. We are they of the serpent and apple, the tree and the dove; the prayers of the Morning Star are known to us. When the Word was rendered and His body cast into the triumphant dark, our mourning made cold the blazing spheres.

We are exiled Princes; our coins are of a foreign land, and we remember songs that were old when the stars were kindled into being. We have suffered and withstood the Forgetting Wild, and upon our re-membrance have put away childish things. We are Perfect and Immortal; we are flawed and absurd. The banner of our Kingdom was unearthed and its revelation set a cooling balm on a burning world.

34

II. THE GNOSTIC WORLD VIEW

Once upon a time – which is how all such stories begin – was the Void, and the Void was with God, and the Void was God. This is the empty Fullness, of which nothing can be said, for all are ripples on the sea of the Fullness. The Fullness, sensing itself, beheld the divine polarity, the seer and the seen. And then there were two.

The two, desiring again to become one, create a third in their reunion, and so Sophia was the child of the polarity. She yearned above all to create, as she was created, and extending forth she issued seven aeons, each a circle rippling out farther from the center; each circle both a realm and a Ruler, devoid of the primal Spark from which their Mother was made. In turn, these sparkless realms desired their own creatures, and made for themselves the system – the kosmos *– and into it cast all of humanity, to dwell in blindness, for the Rulers were terrible and powerful.*

35

Out of great love for the creatures of the Rulers, Sophia cast herself down from the Fullness, bearing the Sacred Flame that was the impetus of her own generation. This she secreted past the seven rulers of the seven heavens, to conceal herself in the form of a serpent, and dwelt in the Garden that was the prison of ignorance wrought for people of earth. In the Garden was a tree, and in the apple of this tree Sophia cached the Spark, and offered the fruit of the Holy Gnosis to Eve.

Upon awakening to gnosis, *Eve possessed something her creators and captors did not understand, and was restored to her birthright as an aware emanation of the Fullness. In compassion, she offered the fruit to her husband, which angered the Rulers – for awareness of who we truly are and from where we have been cast was forbidden by them.*

There is no God before me, cried their King; whereupon Sophia shed the serpent's skin and revealed Herself, declaring, you are

wrong, Blind One. And the people were free to leave the Garden and find their own way.

Some of the Rulers wept with remorse, asking their Mother to return them to the Fullness that they might take their share of the Spark of the Divine. To these She gave the Sacred Flame, and told them to scatter it among all things in the world, that the people might discover them, and upon discovering, remember their sacred kinship with the Queen of Heaven, and the totality of the Fullness.

Man's consciousness was created to the end that it may (1) recognize its descent from a higher unity; (2) pay due and careful regard to this source; (3) execute its commands intelligently and responsibly and; (4) thereby afford the psyche as a whole the optimum degree of life and development.

- Carl Gustav Jung

1. **Who we really are is eternal and immortal;** we're not defined by our bodies or our gender or our horoscopes or our nationalities. Our responsibility is to be integral to this infinite core of being, in ourselves and others. The material universe is temporary and limited, but our real selves are ultimately unconstrained by it.

2. **The system is not the world;** the daily waking reality of economics and politics and bureaucracy, of cruelty and injustice, was not created by the Divine, but by the forces of ignorance and greed. We don't reject rocks and trees and flowers and sex, we reject an unjust system imposed upon these things. This system forces us to feel separated from God, when the reality is that this separation is just an illusion. The system doesn't like to be understood in this

way; it thinks it should be in charge, and our divinity and our humanity should take a back seat to "the way of the world". In this way the system is adversarial to the Gnostic. We see some others "worshipping" this system, as though it were the true God.

3. Faith will not save us from the system; we have to first have *gnosis* – enlightenment – and then understand how our own Divine Spark relates to the world around us. Gnosticism is an experiential, not creedal, religion - you can't simply announce that you agree with a list of ideas and be saved from the illusion of our separation from God. Real salvation requires a critical, inquisitive mind and a compassionate and accommodating heart. We need wit and sorrow and joy and silence and deep questions.

4. Wisdom is in the world and wants to be known; the gifts of our intuition and imagination are not secondary in our efforts to remember our connection to the Infinite Divine. So the practices and approaches of what has generally been referred to as "mysticism" are at the heart of the Gnostic's journey. Dreams and fairy tales, myth and metaphor, secret and cypher, symbol and poetry comprise the language with which the Gnostic interprets the constant signal from the inbreaking Divine.

> In fact I doubt there is a more decisive moment for
> a thinking being than when the scales fall from
> his eyes and he discovers that he is not an isolated
> unit lost in the cosmic solitudes, and realize that a
> universal will to live converges and is hominised in
> him.
>
> - Pierre Teilhard de Chardin

A Few Terms

When we're learning anything new, from Thai cooking to cultivating roses, there's always a small knot of terminology to deal with. When we deal with the realm of spirituality and religion, where the meaning of these terms change over time, this can be even more challenging. "Soul" and "spirit" and "redemption" can be slippery terms because of centuries of misuse, confusion and curious choices of translation. Gnostic terminology is even more challenging as most of it tends to stay in the original Greek.

Here is a very brief introduction to some of the trickier words we're likely to encounter when learning about how Gnostics view the world.

PLEROMA

The Pleroma is "The Fullness"; God ineffable and infinite, too big to fit into one idea or literary character. The Fullness is not the King James Version "God of Abraham", or the Goddess, or a Zeus/Jupiter judgmental figure with beard who answers prayers and punishes the wicked, because each of these ideas serves one time or one culture and is ultimately divisive. For this reason the Pleroma is sometimes referred to as "the God above god." Nothing can truly be divided from God, but we can easily be deceived into believing that we are. Escaping this deception is the entire purpose of Gnosticism.

> He is too great to be called by the name "God." His is hidden, yet obvious everywhere. He is bodiless, yet embodied in everything. There is nothing that he is not. He has no name, because all names are His name. He is the unity in all things, so we must know him by all names and call everything "God."
> –Hermes Trimegistus

It is he who created the entirety and the entirety is in him.

> –*Gospel of Truth*

The Father of all contains all things, and that there is nothing whatever outside of the Pleroma.

> – Valentinus, second century
> Gnostic teacher

So God is boundless time and outside of time, boundless space and outside of space, the Mystery of the infinite and the suddenness of rain on your upturned palm. This idea is known as panentheism: that God is the Universe, but is not contained by the Universe.

The Pleroma is both beginning and end of the created beings. It pervadeth them, as the light of the sun everywhere pervadeth the air. Although the Pleroma prevadeth altogether, yet hath created being no share thereof, just as wholly transparent body becometh neither light nor dark through the light which pervadeth it. We are, however, the Pleroma itself, for we are a part of the eternal and the infinite.

> – Jung, *Seven Sermons to the Dead*

EMANATION

Drop a smooth stone in still water, and understand that all of it – the stone, the water, and the act of dropping – is the Pleroma. This idea of wavelength, of contraction and expansion resulting in all creation, is shared with the mystical Jewish idea of *Tzimtzum*. Everything flows out – *emanates* – from the Fullness.

The first splash of the stone creates a polarity; before the splash, and after the splash. Potential and actual. Female and male. Yin and Yang. This pairing is known as the *Barbelon*. The next ripple out, the first emanation of this stone-dropping event is Sophia, Goddess of Wisdom. The next several ripples are Wisdom's errant children, the intangible "powers that be". Further out still, the ripples represent the world in which we live. And finally, the ripples are us, and from us our ideas and inventions and imaginings. The Gnostic asks, can the waves be separated from water itself, from the stone-event which set it in motion? This view sees the universe and all creation as more verb than noun; as a process rather than a product.

> Their begetting is like a process of extension, as the Father extends himself to those whom he loves, so that those who have come forth from him might become him as well.
>
> – *The Tripartite Tractate*

41

AEON

From a Greek word implying "eternity", the Aeons can be understood as angelic forces: emanated aspects of God, like multiple facets of a single gem. In Gnostic mythology, all the major characters are Aeons: from Sophia who is Wisdom, the Logos/Christ, to Adam and Eve. While these characters are persons (literally "masks" in Greek), they can be best understood psychologically as influences upon human experience.

ABRAXAS

> "The bird is struggling out of the egg.
> The egg is the world. Whoever wants to be born
> must first destroy a world. The bird is flying to God.
> The name of the God is called Abraxas."
>
> – Hermann Hesse, *Demian*

We have numerous surviving carved gems of the classical period bearing prayers for protection. These gems are often illustrated with a bizarre chimera of a creature known as Abraxas, or Abrasax.

The enigmatic figure of a pagan god, with a rooster's head, the torso of a man, and serpents for legs, seems an unlikely depiction of a superpersonal, Platonist "infinite". But in the symbolism of this character, Abraxas, is a visual code for the seven visible planets, the cycles of the sun, and the 365 days of the year. Abraxas appears as an iconic teaching tool for the processes of the universe and our place in it, and this icon is not worshipped as God any more than were the stained glass windows in medieval cathedrals.

As the rooster heralds the dawn, Abraxas is the clarion call to awaken. His legs are the serpents of ancient wisdoms; his chariot the journey forward into understanding. He bears the *aegis* shield of tradition, but also the flail of challenge, of inquiry. Abraxas is a figure deep out of our dreams, out of the current of archetypal symbolism.

> He is a god whom ye knew not, for mankind forgot it. We name it by its name ABRAXAS. It is more indefinite still than god and devil. That god may be distinguished from it, we name god HELIOS or sun. Abraxas is effect. Nothing standeth opposed to it but the ineffective; hence its effective nature freely unfoldeth itself.

The ineffective is not, therefore resisteth not. Abraxas standeth above the sun and above the devil. It is improbable probability, unreal reality. Had the Pleroma a being, Abraxas would be its manifestation.

It is the effective itself, nor any particular effect, but effect in general.

– Jung, Seven Sermons to the Dead

SOPHIA

Yet among the mature we do speak of Sophia, though it is not the Sophia of this Aeon or of the Archons, who are doomed to perish. But we speak of the Holy Sophia, secret and hidden, which God decreed before the Aeons for our glory. None of the Archons understood this.

– St. Paul, Corninthians 2: 6-8

43

Sophia ("Wisdom") is the first Aeon. She is the personification of the Holy Spirit; in Jewish mysticism she is the *Shekhina* or Presence of God. The restoration of Sophia as the Divine Feminine to a place of prominence in Western spirituality addresses a prolonged poverty in our culture.

The myth of Sophia was well known to the philosophers – literally "lovers of Sophia" – and winds its way through Greek and Jewish and Christian understanding; In the Gnostic myth, it is Sophia who creates the first error by emanating the Rulers, or Archons, who in turn create us – not as an act of creative love, but to enslave us by blinding us to the Light of the Pleroma. Sophia realizes Her mistake, takes pity on the creatures of Her children, and descends through the layers which veil us from Heaven to instill within us the Spark of the Divine; the gift of liberating *gnosis*. Upon entering the world governed by the Archons, She becomes lost and forgetful, requiring the Logos to incarnate and rescue Her, restoring Her to Her throne in the *Bythos*, the Profundity.

For centuries before the advent of Christianity, the idea of the Divine Bride and Bridegroom was predominant throughout the diverse cultures of the Holy Land. Inanna and Demuzi, Isis and Osiris, Yahweh and Asherah. It was natural, if not inevitable, for early Christians to incorporate these archetypes in order to convey their Mysteries. The identification of Christ and Mary Magdalene as the Logos and Sophia, Word and Wisdom, stood in the center of the early Christian experience.

This is a story. True not because it happened, but true because it keeps happening. Sophia stands before us in the story of Eve, offering the fruit of *gnosis* to her husband. She greets us in the story of Norea, wife of Noah; in Mary Magdalene, and her later depiction as "Maid Marian". We pursue her as the Holy Grail. We *need* this story, of Wisdom held in the world, redeeming us through insight, through love.

> I am She
> that is the natural
> mother of all things,
> mistress and governess
> of all the elements,
> the initial progeny of worlds,
> chief of the powers divine,
> Queen of all that are in the otherworld,
> the principal of them
> that dwell above,
> manifested alone

and under one form
of all the Gods and Goddesses.
            – Lucius Apuleius

ARCHON

"Ruler"; one of the Aeons emanated by Sophia without the
Light of the Pleroma. In later Gnostic texts, the Archons
are identified with the planets, and with the fatalism of
astrology. The "seven heavens" are ruled by the "seven stars"
in the sky, who attempt to rob us of our free will by trapping
us in predestination. To early Gnostics, the tale of the
exorcism of seven demons from Mary Magdalene is a signal
of her Gnostic liberation. Psychologically, the Archons
can be understood by those forces which keep us in the
artificially constructed system; the false reality of television
and titillation and corruption and consumerism and greed.
The Archons are "the powers that be"; all those ideas which
separate us from living wholly and truthfully, from social
justice, from compassion.

45

> Jesus said, Judas, your star has led you astray... I
> have taught you about the error of the stars.
>   – *Gospel of Judas*

> For our struggle is not against flesh and blood, but
> against the Rulers, against Authorities, against the
> Powers of this dark world and against the spiritual
> forces of evil in the heavenly realms.
>   – St. Paul

DEMIURGE

> A shape with lion body and the head of a man,
> A gaze blank and pitiless as the sun,
> Is moving its slow thighs, while all about it
> Reel shadows of the indignant desert birds.
> The darkness drops again; but now I know
> That twenty centuries of stony sleep
> were vexed to nightmare by a rocking cradle,
> And what rough beast, its hour come round at last,
> Slouches towards Bethlehem to be born?
>
> – WB Yeats, *The Second Coming*

The Demiurge is the "Half-Shaper": Chief of the Archons. He's a problematic figure, as scholars have tried in the past to say that Gnosticism is somehow "about" him. The difficulty with that is that he appears in very few Gnostic texts, and frequently serves different roles. Reading the early Gnostics and deciding that the Demiurge is definitive is like reading the bible's numerous tales of stoning and crucifixion and deciding that is about capital punishment.

In the earlier Platonist texts, the Demiurge is an angel, a benevolent figure who gives us flowers and trees and songbirds. In the darker Sethian material he is an insane dictator bent on deceiving humanity into accepting him as the one true Deity; essentially Satan masquerading as God. While it would be tidy for the purposes of classification if the early Gnostics had found the Demiurge as interesting as later scholars, he's really not as important as some would make it appear. Regardless, at no point is he a creator, *per se*: he is a craftsman, an organizer – all the "stuff" of the universe pre-exists him, and he organizes it in its current form. The carpenter does not make the wood: The librarian is not the author.

In Gnostic myth, the Demiurge declares to Adam and Eve that he is in fact the Supreme God. Sophia, secreted away in the Garden as the serpent, reveals Herself and chastises the Demiurge for his deception and arrogance.

> Now the Archon who is weak has three names.
> The first name is Yaltabaoth ("child"), the second is Saklas ("fool"), and the third is Samael("blind one"). And he is impious in his arrogance which is in him. For he said, 'I am God and there is no other God beside me,' for he is ignorant of his strength, the place from which he had come.
>
> – *The Secret Book of John*

The Demiurge serves as a warning to us: He is the power of our own Divinity unchecked by our compassion; he is our worship of simplistic ideas and the temptation to rely on a Santa Claus-type God who grants us cancer-cures and winning lottery tickets if only we humble ourselves sufficiently. He is the "false god" of our own construction. In the works of William Blake, the Demiurge is referred to as "Old Nobodaddy". In 2 *Corinthians* St. Paul calls him "the god of this world", and in Ephesians he is referred to as "*kosmokrator*", the Ruler of the System.

47

LOGOS

> In the beginning was the Logos, and the Logos was with God, and the Logos was God. He was with God in the beginning. Through him all things were made; without him nothing was made that has been made. In him was life, and that life was the light of men. The light shines in the darkness, but the darkness has not understood it.
>
> – *The Gospel of John*

Gnostic Christians, such as the authors of the prologue to the *Gospel of John*, viewed Christ as an expression of the *Logos*, the Greek idea of "the rightness of things" or "natural law". Later this term came to imply the personification of mind, or reason. It must be understood that the character of Jesus in Gnostic literature is just that: a character. He is presented not as an historic rabbi presented verbatim in an historic chronicle, but as an archetype – a component of the reader, your personal, inner initiator into the Mystery. The Gnostic does not argue, for example, that in *The Gospel of Judas* Jesus actually said a particular phrase to Judas some 2,000 years ago; rather, that this wisdom is being communicated to you, right now. These stories don't matter because they happened, *they matter because they are beautiful.*

Rather than being limited to the Jesus stories, the Gnostic Christ is a kind of Divine Twin for each of us: the part of you which resides in the Fullness. Your own future enlightened, spiritually-revealed Self; eternal, immortal, and burdened with a terrible and awesome responsibility to awaken and serve.

> I am established. I am redeemed, and I redeem my soul from this Aeon and from all that comes from it, in the name of IAO, who redeemed his soul unto the redemption in Christ, the living one.
>
> – Valentinus

In the *Naassene Psalm*, Jesus observes from Heaven the plight of Sophia, lost among the Archons in her rescue attempt of humanity;

Clad in the shape of a deer she is worn away with
death's slavery.
Now she has mastery and glimpses light: now she is
plunged in misery and weeps.
Now she is mourned, and her self rejoices.
Now she weeps and is finally condemned.
Now she is condemned and finally dies.
 And now she reaches the point where hemmed in
by evil, she knows no way out.
Misled, she has entered a labyrinth.
Then Jesus said " Behold, Father, she wanders the
earth pursued by evil.
Far from thy Breath she is going astray.
She is trying to flee bitter Chaos, and does not know
how she is to escape.
Send me forth, o Father, therefore, and I, bear-
ing the seal shall descend and wander all Aeons
through, all mysteries reveal.
I shall manifest the forms of the gods and teach
them the secrets of the holy way which I call *Gnosis*.

THE GNOSTIC EVE

I am thou and thou art I,
and wherever thou art, there am I,
and I am sown in all things;
and whence thou wilt, thou gatherest me,
but when thou gatherest me,
then gatherest thou thyself.
　　　 – *Gospel of Eve*

Few things give lie to the claim that Gnostics "hated the
flesh" better than the portrayal of Eve in Gnostic scripture,

in which she is an enlightened heroine. While she is responsible, ultimately, for the material incarnation of all who come after her, she is also a "luminous woman" and an agent of liberation; she – as "instructor" – gives Adam the true life of *gnosis* thus making him truly alive. The Origin of the World invokes the very physical imagery of pregnancy, of midwifery and labor, and yet The Great Mother is shown to be a Force, an Aeon, spiritually superior to those who would try to constrain her.

> After the day of rest, Sophia sent her daughter Zoe ("life"), being called Eve, as an instructor, in order that she might make Adam, who had no soul, arise, so that those whom he should engender might become containers of light. When Eve saw her male counterpart prostrate, she had pity upon him, and she said, "Adam! Become alive! Arise upon the earth!" Immediately her word became accomplished fact. For Adam, having arisen, suddenly opened his eyes. When he saw her, he said, "You shall be called 'Mother of the Living'. For it is you who have given me life."

> Then the Archons were informed that their modelled form was alive and had arisen, and they were greatly troubled.
> They sent seven archangels to see what had happened. They came to Adam. When they saw Eve talking to him, they said to one another, "What sort of thing is this luminous woman?
> For she resembles that likeness which appeared to us in the light. Now come, let us lay hold of her and cast her seed into her, so that when she becomes soiled she may not be able to ascend into her light.

Rather, those whom she bears will be under our charge. But let us not tell Adam, for he is not one of us. Rather let us bring a deep sleep over him. And let us instruct him in his sleep to the effect that she came from his rib, in order that his wife may obey, and he may be lord over her."

Then Eve, being a force, laughed at their decision.

– *The Origin of the World*

Hopefully this has helped you navigate some of the density associated with Gnostic myth and symbolism, but the most important part of this process is actually *eisegesis* (reading in) rather than *exegesis* (reading out). All these myths are merely tools, such as the letters of the alphabet or musical notation. Each symbol – from poetic metaphor to bizarre pagan godforms – functions in a way similar to coins and sticks in the *I Ching*; nothing particularly significant in and of themselves, but in combination provide an opportunity for contemplation and inspiration.

51

GNOSTICISM AND ORTHODOXY

	Orthodoxy	Gnosticism
God	Abrahamic, personal	Platonist, superpersonal
Christ	Historic, Son of God, exclusive, external	Archetypal, exemplar, inclusive, internal
Salvation	faith	enlightenment
Humanity	Contaminated by Original Sin	Sparks of the Divine
Scripture	Authoritative	Myth and poetry
The Body	Positive definitive "you are your body"	Positive temporary "you are not your body"
Eve	Cause of Original Sin	First Gnostic Saint
Source of Evil	Satan	ignorance
Critical value	obedience	curiosity

Enlighten your mind... Light the lamp within you.
Knock on yourself as if upon a door and walk upon
yourself as upon a straight road. For if you walk on
the road, it is impossible for you to go astray. Open
the door for you so that you may know what it is.

–Silvanus

III. PRAXIS

Summer night, 1986. Restless and unable to sleep, I go for a midnight walk along Sunset Beach in Vancouver. I remember the reflection of the stars on the water, people crabbing in the gentle Pacific surf, trousers rolled like eliot.

A large heron, alighting to the grey sand, glides past my head, wingtip missing by millimetres. And in that sound that is not a sound, more a simple compression of warm night air, I hear the Voice of the Divine, and I know*. For me it is Basho's frog, or the clack of a broom against a wooden chair. I hear the tumblers of the universe roll and click into place.*

What I knew *in that moment is the suddenness, the immediacy of magic in the world; constant, present, incessant, infinite and luminous.*

55

Gnosticism is a contemplative, sacramental and creative religion; in contemplation it is intensely personal, intimate, challenging and disciplined; at the same time in a sacramental setting it is romantic, imaginative, poetic, and joyous. The question "What do Gnostics do?" can roughly be answered by examining the practices of these three interweaving paths.

Contemplation

The practice of mindfulness involves constantly trying to keep in mind through our actions, words, decisions, or reactions if we're being the person we're supposed to be; if we're making at least our corner of our world a better place. Can I be less antagonistic to the person who is getting on my nerves? Am I honestly being respectful of the people around me? Am I serving the Sacred Flame in myself and others, right here, right now?

We fail at this all the time, but we prepare for that failure, and we keep going.

This raises the question of sin, an idea which still dominates our superficially secular culture. At its root, it denotes lack, a shortfall or insufficiency. The Greek idea of sin literally means "missing the mark", as in archery, aiming for the bull's eye and hitting instead an adjacent circle, or the green turf below. It's not a particularly judgmental idea, and actually rather forgiving. *Oops, I missed, try again.* Being aware of when we're less than aware lets us examine the target and correct our aim.

> The aim of life is to live, and to live means to be aware, joyously, drunkenly, serenely, divinely aware.
>
> – Henry Miller

A very simple and common practice is lighting **candles of intention**: Light a candle to express a thought, such as the health of a loved one. Just the act of turning a mental image into a physical action is clarifying and empowering, and the warmth and light are ambient reminders of that thought. It puts "first things first" and aids greatly in focus. There's that feeling of first steps, that however overwhelming the world can be, *I can at least do this.*

Most Gnostics incorporate prayer, but with an intention quite different from how it's usually approached in Western culture. It's never about begging God for favours, but rather it's about invoking the transformative power of living in concert with Wisdom, with God. The transformative assumption in prayer is that there is a way we're supposed to be – more creative, more intimate, braver, fair-minded, compassionate, more spontaneous, adventurous, calmer, rooted, deliberate, responsible, raw – and that we can bring that ideal state to the here and now by listening to *that*

rather than all the competing, clamorous voices that make it easier to be *this*.

If this sounds a little dramatic, remember that you are declaring a revolution, the overthrow of the powers which govern your life in favour of a profound, fundamental shift that unites your Divinity with your humanity. The real question is, if prayer is not radical, political, transformative, sexual, artistic, creative, scary, and intoxicating, then why would you want to have anything to do with it?

Contemplative Prayer

A less demanding, but equally transformative approach to this kind of meditation is contemplative prayer.

Choose a word of significance (*heart, grace, peace, listening*), and sit comfortably. Feet on the floor, palms on your thighs, eyes closed. Silently invoke the word. Don't worry if you're doing this right, or sitting properly, or have chosen the right word. Don't worry at all. Just focus on the word.

Random thoughts will emerge; forgive them, and gently return to the word. You'll find it difficult to keep still; but just breathe, adjust, and return to that point of stillness. Be kind to yourself, as its very easy to become distracted and fall out of that place of calm. At the end of the prayer, just sit silently for a moment, and try to bring some of that stillness into your regular world.

Lectio Divina

A more formal contemplative practice is that of lectio divina (divine reading), first outlined by the third-century Christian Origen, whose teachings – despite being highly critical of the Gnostics – were ironically influenced by Gnosticism.

First, select a passage from something which inspires you. Many of the scriptural selections in this book are suitable for this practice.

Now read the passage out loud, first in a normal voice, and secondly in a slower, more poetic voice. Taste the words in your mouth and feel the vibration in your body. Concentrate on the sound of it, the music of it.

Consider the words silently. Ask yourself what they mean, why the phrasing is how it is, what the phrase is definitely not saying. What did these words mean to the writers and audiences in the time the text was written?

Next, prayerfully invite the Divinity of the passage to reveal itself to you. Slow down, get quiet, and search for the deeper meaning – not intellectually but spiritually.

58

Finally, just sit in silence with the experience of connecting with the message. Don't analyze or insist on any kind of resolution. Just abide with it, like sitting beside a sleeping dog on a porch at sunset.

Other forms of contemplation employed by contemporary Gnostics include Jungian psychology, dream journalling and analysis, and the symbolic practice of tarot. Not seen to be "supernatural", but as rich archetypal starting-points for contemplation, tarot has supporters in orthodox mysticism as well;

> A thinking, praying Christian of unmistakable purity reveals to us the symbols of Christian Hermeticism in its various levels of mysticism, *gnosis* and magic, taking in also the Cabbala and certain elements of astrology and alchemy. These symbols are summarized in the twenty-two "Major Arcana" of the tarot cards. By way of the Major Arcana, the author seeks to lead meditatively into the deeper, all embracing wisdom of the Catholic mystery."
>
> – Hans Urs von Balthazar

THE ALCHEMY OF THE SACRAMENTS

For many modern Gnostics, their practice takes the form of what has been called by Dr. John Plummer the "Independent Sacramental Movement"; a very traditional ritual with vestments, candles, priests, deacons and bishops – albeit with a fiercely independent interpretation of the meaning of all these elements.

Gnosticism has always had a sacramental system; from the original five sacraments of the early Gnostic texts to the Latinized seven sacraments after 1913.

> The Lord did everything in a Mystery, a baptism and a chrism and a eucharist and a redemption and a bridal chamber.
>
> *– Gospel of Philip*

These five sacraments are the "five trees" referred to in the Gospel of Thomas;

> For there are five trees in Paradise for you; they do not change, summer or winter, and their leaves do not fall. Whoever knows them will not taste death
>
> *– Gospel of Thomas 19*

The Eucharist: Everything Wants to Transform

It is in our essential nature that we want to change, to grow – as does everything. The acorn wills to become the oak, the caterpillar the butterfly, the infant the adolescent, the adolescent the adult. Transformation is the natural order of things: But we do have a habit, we errant stars, of getting in our own way.

Alchemy (literally "of Egypt") is the intersection of both the early natural sciences and philosophical inquiry. It is a way of organizing experience around common themes, metaphorically identified as earth, air, fire and water, with spirit as the fifth element, or quintessence. All creation is understood to be composed of and influenced by the nature of these elements, and they correspond to seasons, temperaments, and the wandering stars of the night sky. The medieval alchemists were concerned with the idea of separating, combining and balancing these elements to create transformation; both materially and spiritually.

So the first thing any good Alchemist does is sort out the elements. In the Eucharist we have the host (earth), incense (air), candles (fire), and wine (water) as well as the invocations of the four elemental Archangels to do this (Raphael, Michael, Gabriel, and Uriel). But we need to concentrate the animating force, the quintessence of the Holy Spirit, to give the elements life and meaning.

What this means for each of us is that we need to successfully negotiate between the elemental forces acting upon human experience: the physical, the intellectual, the willful, and the emotional. If these forces are in conflict, it's harder to hear the voice of that Quintessential Spirit. Step one is to sort them out, set them aside, examine and honour them and find some equilibrium.

The uninhabited host is not a "commemorative meal", it's just a cracker. Our aim is to trans-sub-stant-iate (*across-under-standing-ify*) the host by imbuing it with this Fifth Element. We do this through poetry, through ritual psychodrama, through gesture, through music and silence, through myth and beauty. This is how all good transformations are undertaken; how curiosity becomes love, how love becomes life.

The solar initiation of the Eucharist is a real and magical event, and we accomplish it with words that are the origin of "hocus pocus" (*hoc est enim corpus meum*, "this is my body").

This pushes the "root", (*hypostasis* = underlying reality), of the host sideways from the material realm into the mythic realm, so that it can become nourishment for our mythic selves: The Infinite becomes finite, so that the finite may become again Infinite. *Solve et Coagula*. As above, so below.

And this is the miracle of the Mass.

In a 1990 article in *Gnosis* magazine, Charles Upton suggests astronomical/alchemical correspondences to the sacraments, which we shall briefly explore here;

Baptism is the lunar celebration of birth into the circle of community. It speaks to the element of water, of honouring tides, and the washing away of your former identity and celebrates the emergence from the womb of the Mother.

Chrismation is the strengthening of the initiatory intelligence, and relates to a more mature relationship with the Logos (symbolized by the planet Mercury). Whereas the baptismal metaphors are clearly that of physical birth, confirmation speaks to the individuation of the psyche. While baptism is considered a valid sacrament even to those too young to comprehend its significance, confirmation must be undertaken by a reasoned and receptive mind.

Penance is the ritual forgiveness of error committed after baptism. By honestly confronting our errors, and understanding how they interfere with our reunion and betray our own gnosis, the Gnostic undergoes an *agon* – a struggle between those aspects of self which are connected to the Mystery vs. our connections to the ego. This struggle can be seen as an invocation of the forces of the planet Mars. Its purpose is not judgmental but to return to a state of mindfulness and focus.

Matrimony's association with the planet Venus – pagan goddess of love – is obvious, and relates to the Alchemical process of Conjunction. The marriage of two people coming together in a Spiritual context to help make each other more Divine is seen as a parallel to the Bride Chamber of Sophia described in *The Gospel of Philip*.

> Great is the mystery of marriage! For without it, the world would not exist.
>
> *- The Gospel of Philip.*

The structure of **Holy Orders** – order here as in "putting things in order", not "commands" – grants the responsibility of spiritual kingship (associated with Jupiter) upon the ordained, resulting in the expansion of the spiritual resources of the community as a whole. The major orders of deacon, priest and bishop are preceded by the minor orders of doorkeeper, reader, exorcist and acolyte. Some Gnostic churches also offer monastic orders for solitary practitioners who live away from regions served by a parish.

Extreme Unction – sometimes called "last rites" – is associated with the planet Saturn; sphere of Limit, and of Time. As Baptism is Initiation into the powers of life, so is Extreme Unction an Initiation into the powers of death.

Given this richness and complexity of sacramental heritage, it would be easy to assume that most Gnostics place shared worship as an important part of their religious identity. The reality is that there are so few Gnostic parishes that most Gnostics will never attend Mass or be baptized in the name of their own religion. Gnostics are so geographically diverse that few will ever meet a coreligionist. Instead, for most, their path is expressed in contemplation and in creativity: A significant number of Gnostics are artists, writers, musicians, filmmakers, dancers, photographers. The *gnosis* event lends itself equally to artistic expression as it does to participation in the sacraments.

IV. THE LITURGICAL YEAR

CANDLEMAS: FEBRUARY 2

> Bride put her finger in the river
> On the Feast Day of Bride
> And away went the hatching mother of the cold.
> — *Carmina Gadelica*

> She tells her love while half asleep,
> In the dark hours,
> With half-words whispered low:
> As Earth stirs in her winter sleep
> And puts out grass and flowers
> Despite the snow,
> Despite the falling snow.
> – Robert Graves, *She Tells Her Love*

Both of these poems, one ancient, and one modern, speak of the binary facets of nature, and the gentle turning of winter into spring. Rather than stop there at the gates of simple seasonal truth (an hemispheric truth; a half-truth at best), these words invite us to welcome our own thaw – the frozen solidity of surety melting in the Light to the watery yield of *gnosis*.

Traditionally too this is the season of the Bride, the welcoming of Sophia into the Bridal Chamber. Each crocus and daffodil, every quietly triumphant snowdrop calls to Her; calls to the half-asleep-but-waking Wisdom in each of us.

In Gnostic churches this is the traditional day of the blessing of candles used in ritual practice.

VALENTINUS: FEBRUARY 14

In memory of the Gnostic Saint and teacher, Valentinus;

> God came and destroyed the division, and he
> brought the hot Pleroma of love, so that the cold
> may not return.
>> – St. Valentine c.100-153,
>> *The Gospel of Truth*

Valentinus was perhaps the most important Gnostic teacher of the early Christian era. His embrace of the sacred nature of sexuality was in stark contrast to the extreme asceticism and denial of the flesh of the "desert fathers". His writings deftly navigate the currents of classical pagan thought, Christianity, and philosophy. The Valentinians were criticized by the later orthodox for having female clergy, including bishops.

ASH WEDNESDAY - LENT

> Blessèd sister, holy mother,
> spirit of the fountain, spirit
> of the garden,
> Suffer us not to mock ourselves
> with falsehood
> Teach us to care and not to care
> Teach us to sit still
> Even among these rocks,
> Our peace in His will

And even among these rocks
Sister, mother
And spirit of the river,
spirit of the sea,
Suffer me not to be separated

And let my cry come unto Thee.
                    - T.S. Eliot - A*sh Wednesday*

*"Remember that thou art dust and unto dust thou shalt
return."*

For the Gnostic, this isn't maudlin, nor is it a sugar-coating
our material existence. There is a tremendous virtue in
contemplation of our impermanence, and the resulting
detachment. The danger, of course, is the tempting slide into
nihilism:

> "... our body will be ashes and our spirit will be
> poured abroad like unresisting air.
>
> Even our name will be forgotten in time, and no
> one will recall our deeds. So our life will pass away
> like the traces of a cloud, and will be dispersed like
> a mist pursued by the sun's rays and overpowered
> by its heat.
>
> For our lifetime is the passing of a shadow; and our
> dying cannot be deferred because it is fixed with a
> seal; and no one returns."
>   – *The Book of Sophia*, Chapter 2

In *The Book of Sophia* these are the words of the unwise,
who court despair at worst and frivolousness at best. What
they learn in the remainder of the text is that, yes, earthly

attachment is fleeting, but the point of existence remains through the love and alliance of Wisdom:

> Resplendent and unfading is Sophia, and she is readily perceived by those who love her, and found by those who seek her.

MONTSEGUR DAY / STE. ESCLARMONDE: MARCH 16

In this day in 1244 CE some two hundred Gnostics - the last holdouts of a year-long siege - proceeded solemnly from the gates of their ancient stronghold and into the waiting fires of Catholic France. These *Parfaits* or clerics of the Cathar religion were flowers of a culture centuries ahead of their murderers in literacy, medicine, mathematics, and in what was later to be regarded as civil and human rights. They practiced pacifism, sexual equality, contraception, and vegetarianism; believed in re-incarnation to a degree, and marched serenely into martyrdom.

The massacre at Montsegur was part of the Albigensian Crusade, a vicious campaign waged by the armies of the Roman Church upon the people and culture of the Languedoc in what is now southern France. The cities of Europe were emptied of those willing to slaughter in the name of the Bishop of Rome, for forgiveness of any sins and for whatever land they could seize. Montsegur tore the heart out of the Cathar nation, but the Crusade did not end until the fall of Quéribus in 1255.

Some of the surviving eleven knights and 1,500 men-at-arms, along with 500 or so civilians, were allowed to live after renouncing their faith, all properties and any future rights. But many, on the eve of the fall of the fortress of Montsegur, chose instead the *Consolamentum*, the ordination of the Parfaits, and certain incineration.

A generation before the fall of Montsegur, the father of the Inquisition, St. Dominic, came to Cathar country to denounce their heresy and debate their parfaits. Legend has it that after being defeated in one such debate by a Cathar noblewoman and parfait, Ste. Esclarmonde de Foix, Dominic cried "Go home to your spinning, woman!" Legend further recounts that when the Inquisition came to arrest Ste. Esclarmonde to burn her at the stake that she transformed into a dove and flew away.

Today we honour the Cathar's sacrifice and dedication to the Truth, and their surrender to it.

> "Holy Father, rightful Lord of the faithful souls, Who never erred, Who never lied, Who always followed the rightful course, Who never doubted lest we should accept death in the world of the wrong god; as we do not belong to this world and this world is not ours - teach us what You know and love what You love."

ST. GABRIEL THE ARCHANGEL
MARCH 24

Lighting a blue candle:

> In the name of Light descending, we summon Gabriel, Lord of Water, Heavenly Herald, who didst bring glad tidings to Our Blessed Lady. May this Chamber be guarded and our acts here witnessed. Come mighty Gabriel, and grace us with thy presence.

ST. JOAN OF ARC: MARCH 30

In memory of the Gnostic Saint Joan of Arc, whose *gnosis* (through a vision of the Archangel Michael) led her people to freedom, even at the cost of her own destruction.

> White lily with red rose
> We wed,
> And with secret, prophetic dream
> We attain eternal Truth.
>
> Speak the prophetic word!
> Quickly cast your pearls into the cup;
> Now bind our Dove
> With new coils of the old Serpent.
>
> The free heart hurts not!
> Should the Dove fear Promethean fire?
> The pure Dove is calm
> In the flaming coils of the mighty Serpent.
>
> Sing about violent tempests!
> In violent tempests we find repose;
> For white lily with red rose
> We wed.
>
>   – Vladimir Soloviev, Gnostic Poet

PALM SUNDAY

> The images are manifest to man, but the light in
> them remains concealed in the image of the light of
> the Father.
>
> – *Gospel of Thomas*

This is the day of the declaration of the light, in mindful
provocation – in outright defiant challenge – of archonic
Authority. This is the day of knowing who we are, and
wherein we have been cast; the day of Identity and
Identification.

We each of us today cease to conceal our light, knowing that
we are a beacon guiding our enemies – the multitude that is
our attachment, our jealousies, our petty preoccupations – to
the inevitable destruction of what we know as our lives. The
Light of Sophia encourages us – literally *gives us the heart*
– to step forward into our identity.

71

Do we need laurels for this? Do we need medals and
corporate helicopters to speed us to a satellite-fed press
conference? No, we need our humility, our simplicity. We
ride into the welcoming throng of Jerusalem on an ass.

The donkey is our everyday self: it is this which transports
the Christ-in-us forward into the City of Wholeness,
Jerusalem. The pedestrian nature of the vessel in no way
diminishes the Divinity of the wine.

This is our hour; the Rulers will in turn have theirs. Soon
there will be a surge in the tide of darkness, and all our hope
will be undone; our lives and selves are to be flensed away
by overwhelming archonic force. But not yet.

The Gnostics believed in two temporal ages: the first or present evil; the second or future benign. The first age was the Age of Iron. It is represented by a Black Iron Prison. It ended in August 1974 and was replaced by the Age of Gold, which is represented by a Palm Tree Garden.

> – Philip K. Dick,
> *Tractates Cryptica Scriptura*

GOOD FRIDAY

For more than four thousand years, Western religion has recognized this time of year as the seeming triumph of darkness over light, of despair over hope.

Set has overthrown Wesir, and cast him into the rivers. The Empire has murdered the Logos upon the stauros like a criminal. We are lost and undone.

This blackness is to embraced, confronted, transmuted, and then put aside as the faint glimmer of hope blossoms into the full flower of Spring and the Renewal of Life. In the Darkness is encoded the promise Light.

We have Aset to find the scattered body of the Lord, we have the Magdalene to witness the Resurrection. The water of the Incarnate is soon to be the heady wine of the Immutable Spirit.

But not yet.

> I would be saved, and I would save.
> I would be loosed, and I would loose.
>
> I would be wounded, and I would wound.
> I would be born, and I would bear.
>
> I would eat, and I would be eaten.
> I would hear, and I would be heard.
>
> I would be thought, being wholly thought.
> I would be washed, and I would wash.
>
> Grace danceth. I would pipe; dance ye all.
> I would mourn: lament ye all.
> *–The Acts of John*

EASTER MONDAY

And there you have it. The Spring Equinox, the Full Moon,
the First Day of the Sun, and the Logos is restored to us,
Immortal and incorruptible, as is the spark of Divinity
within us all.

> This libation is Yours, Father,
> For You, coming forth from Your son,
> Coming forth before the Logos.
> I come to bring You the Eye of the Logos to refresh
> Your heart.
> I have brought it to You, under Your sandals;
> This libation, which comes forth from You.

74

The living water. The Father from the Son. Lux ex Tenebris.
We Know this. We have always Known this.

> That which is called the Christian religion existed
> among the ancients, and never did not exist, from
> the beginnings of the human race until Christ came
> in the flesh, at which time the true religion, which
> already existed, began to be called Christianity.
> - St. Augustine, *Retractions*

TERRA MATER: APRIL 22

The earth is at the same time mother,
She is mother of all that is natural,
mother of all that is human.
She is the mother of all,
for contained in her are the seeds of all.
The earth of humankind contains all moistness,
all verdancy, all germinating power.
It is in so many ways fruitful.
All creation comes from it.
Yet it forms not only the basic raw material for
humankind,
but also the substance of the Incarnation.

       – Hildegard von Bingen

BELTANE: MAY 1

Come, oh souls, to this ship of Light!

My most beloved soul, who is happy and noble,
where have you gone? Return!
Awake, dear soul, from the sleep of drunkenness
into which you have fallen!
Look upon the foes, see how they prepare death all
around you.
Reach your home, the heavenly earth created by the
Word,
Where you were in the beginning.

> – Bardesanes, *Hymns to the Soul*

76

ST. JULIAN OF NORWICH: MAY 8

In memory of the Gnostic Julian of Norwich, visionary and
Saint. She is generally regarded as the first female author in
the English language.

The passing life of the senses doesn't lead
to knowledge of what our Self is.
When we clearly see what our Self is,
then we shall truly *know* our Lord God in great joy."

> – Mother Julian of Norwich (1342 - 1416)

PENTECOST

This is the legacy of the ancient feast of the Egyptian god-form Khnum (*kneph*, spirit or breath) dating from around 1550 BCE. Khnum is regarded as one of the oldest of the *netjeru*, the names or articulated conceptions of the divine.

Unlike a primitive storm god or mountain god or cow god, Khnum demonstrates an abstract awareness of the divinity of life. As long as something breathes, it has a spark, an indwelling magic, that goes away when the breathing stops. But that breath is seen to survive - leave the body yes, but endure. Hence the idea of breath evolving into the idea of Spirit. The Pneuma Hagion.

So Pentecost is the season in which the Western Religion, the Holy (whole) and Catholic (universal) Church, celebrates the descent of the Pneuma. The story says, don't worry, the physical Jesus you knew and loved is gone, but the deep magic, the ubiquitous and eternal Holy Spirit, is with you right now, bringing Inspiration and Comfort. This is clearly an allegory of Initiation.

Christians begin with the story of a carpenter from Nazareth, who ate bread and wore sandals and existed in a time and place. This is a simple introductory framework for Wisdom in the form of parables. Pentecost speaks to the next stage of Initiation: the Jesus you knew was a myth, a composite, not an historical person, but a necessary degree in your Initiation into the Mysteries. You are now ready for a more adult, abstract idea of God; you can put away childish things.

As in conception, from the Father issues forth the Seed (the Logos) to take root in the Mother (the Spirit, which is feminine in both Greek and Hebew), wherein it is nurtured and matured. So too is the process of inspiration and maturation of the Gnostic.

There is among our tenets one to which I shall call particular attention: the tenet of feminine salvation. The work of the Father has been accomplished, that of the Son as well. There remains that of the Spirit, which alone is capable of bringing about the final salvation of humanity on earth and thereby, of laying the way for the reconstitution of the Spirit. Now the Spirit, the Paraclete, corresponds to what the divine partakes of a feminine nature, and our teachings state explicitly that this is the only facet of the godhead that is truly accessible to our mind.

- Fabre des Essarts (Tau Synesius),
Gnostic Bishop, 1908

ST. URIEL THE ARCHANGEL: JUNE 22

Lighting a green candle:

In the name of Light returning, we summon Uriel, Dark Lord of Earth, who bringest all at last unto the Nether Shore, Companion of all who offer up their lives in the defense of others, guard this Chamber and witness the acts here taken. Come, mighty Uriel, and grace us with thy presence.

ST. JOHN THE BAPTIST: JUNE 24

> The people were in expectation, and all men mused
> in their hearts of John, whether he were the Christ,
> or not.
>
> – *Luke* 3:15

In Acts 19, Paul is said to travel to Ephesus, only to discover
that a community of followers of John the Baptist has
already been established. These people have been identified
as Mandaeans, a Gnostic religion which survives to the
present day.

The name "John" is a relatively recent interpretation of the
Hebrew name "Yohanen", meaning "of the waters". There is
an etymological connection to Oannes, the Sumerian god
of initiation and enlightenment. In ancient art, Oannes is
depicted with a fish-head crown, reminiscent of a modern
bishop's mitre. The figure of John the Baptist can be
understood as an expression of this Initiator archetype.

John proclaims in the nights and says:

> Through my Father's discourses I give light and
> through the praise of the Man, my creator. I have
> freed my soul from the world and from the works
> that are hateful and wrong. The Seven Archons put
> question to me, the Dead who have not seen Life,
> and they said unto me; "In whose strength dost thou
> stand there, and with whose praise dost thou make
> proclamation?"
>
> Thereupon gave to them answer: I stand in the
> strength of my Father and with the praise of the

Man, my creator. I have built no house in Judea,
I have set up no throne in Jerusalem. I have not
loved the wreath of the roses, not commerce with
lovely women. I have not loved the deficiency , not
loved the cup of the drunkards. I have loved no food
of the body, and envy has found no place in me.
I have not forgotten my night-prayer, not forgotten the wondrous Jordan. I have not forgotten my
baptizing, not forgotten my pure sign. I have not
forgotten Sun-day, and the Day`s evening has not
condemned me. I have not forgotten Shilmai and
Nidbai, who dwell in the House of the Mighty. They
clear me and let me ascend; they know no fault, no
defect in me.

When John said this, Life rejoiced over him greatly.
The Seven sent him their greeting and the Twelve
made obeisance before him.

> – *The Book of John the Baptist*

FEAST OF THE MAGDALENE: JULY 22

Peter said to Mary, Sister we know that the Savior
loved you more than the rest of woman. Tell us the
words of the Savior which you remember which you
know, but we do not, nor have we heard them.

Mary answered and said, What is hidden from you
I will pro- claim to you. And she began to speak to
them these words:

I, she said, I saw the Lord in a vision and I said to
Him, Lord I saw you today in a vision. He answered
and said to me,
Blessed are you that you did not waver at the sight
of Me. For where the mind is there is the treasure.

– Gospel of Mary Magdalene

The identification with Mary Magdalene is extremely
popular among contemporary Gnostics. As the first of the
apostles to witness of the Resurrection, she is seen as co-
equal with Christ and the first to truly understand the post-
incarnational aspect of the Logos. In this role of initiated
initiator, she is celebrated as an aspect of Sophia Herself.

ST. JOSEPH OF ARIMETHEA: JULY 31

May my house be at peace in this time of war. May I have a voice in this time of oppressive silence. May I have love in this time of immense loneliness. May I have justice in this time of cruelty, democracy in this age of despots.

May I remember that I am blessed; that in my life the Grail may be be unveiled and championed openly. This openness is not to be taken for granted, and on this day we are called to be mindful of those who have protected and concealed the Grail in their time.

St. Joseph of Arimathea is said to have smuggled the Secret, at great peril and in a time of relentless persecution, to conceal the Treasure in the welcoming mists of the fringes of Empire. He invites us to reflect on and honour those who today shelter the chalice beneath the pall.

ASSUMPTION OF SOPHIA: AUGUST 15

Resplendent and unfading is Sophia, and she is
readily perceived by those who love her, and found
by those who seek her.

For Sophia, the artificer of all, taught me. For in her
is a spirit intelligent, holy, unique, manifold, subtle,
agile, clear, unstained, certain, Not baneful, loving
the good, keen, unhampered, beneficent, kindly,
firm, secure, tranquil, all-powerful, all-seeing, and
pervading all spirits, though they be intelligent,
pure and very subtle.

For Sophia is mobile beyond all motion, and she
penetrates and pervades all things by reason of her
purity.

For she is an aura of the might of God and a pure
effusion of the glory of the Almighty; therefore
nought that is sullied enters into her.

For she is the refulgence of eternal light, the spot-
less mirror of the power of God, the image of his
goodness.

And she, who is one, can do all things, and renews
everything while herself perduring; And passing into holy souls from age to age, she produces
friends of God and prophets.

For there is nought God loves, be it not one who
dwells with Sophia.

For she is fairer than the sun and surpasses every constellation of the stars. Compared to light, she takes precedence; for that, indeed, night supplants, but wickedness prevails not over Sophia.

– *The Book of Sophia*

DESCENT OF SOPHIA: SEPTEMBER 8

Homesick. We have this old, old word, simple as a wooden spoon, to sketch a small picture of a bruised heart. A somewhere that is not here alone offers the paraclete of hearth and familiarity, easier laughter, little, easier loves. Here is only allogenic discord, harsh and overbright. Where *there* is a sigh, *here* is the sharp intake of breath, as upon the bruising of a shin. A scraped knuckle, a rock in the sandal. An incessant, weird otherness. *I do not belong here*, says Homesick, our old companion, our weary traveller.

Into such a wilderness wanders the Magna Mater, Regina Coeli. She embarks on this journey, far from the Green Country, armed with only the Right, and a pocketful of seeds. She is aware of course, of the risks of this place – the Goblin Market hungers and poison apples of amnesia – for She Herself is Wisdom. But She comes here willingly; it is Her offspring that crafted this landscape, made little prisons for its inhabitants out of words, coins, clocks, and little fears. She is able to respond, therefore She is *responsible*, and it is this that draws Her onward, proudly through the desolate waste, the seeds in her palm warm from stolen Promethean fire.

85

Homesick. Such a mousey little word to encompass an enormity of distance, of loss. Every step a forgetting, a drowsy sorrow. Not a fanfare-heralded overthrow on a noble battlefield, just a mournful keening of empty wind, an undaunted shuffling through a cooling grey desert.

The seeds of Wisdom, though, they find us. Little scraps, fragments of Her, ablaze in the dark. We are the keepers of such seeds, Knights of the Lost Queen. Achamoth. Today She is not Our Lady, Queen of Heaven. Today we see Her as the sojourner, the Fallen, and we honour Her sacrifice, and the heartbreak of her Fall.

ST. HILDEGARD OF BINGEN: SEPTEMBER 17

O Holy Fire,
paraclete of the spirit,
life force of all creation,
holiness you are in living form
You are a holy ointment
for perilous injuries
You are holy in cleansing
the fetid wound.

O breath of holiness
o fire of loving
o sweet taste in the breast
you fill the heart
with the good aroma of virtues.

O fountain of purity
in whom it is considered
that God collected the lost
and the damned saved.

O robe of life and hope for the companions
our brothers all of the church
and the belt of honesty
save the blessed.

Caring for all those
who are held down by enemies
and break the chains
whom the Divine will save and free.

O path of strength
that enters all places
in the high places and in the plains
and in all the depths
you call and unify all.

From you the smoke flows,
the ether flies,
jewels given their qualities
water streams shown their way
and earth made green and fresh.

You always teach comprehending
by inspirational wisdom with joy.

Praise be to you,
who is the sound of praise,
and joy of life, hope and noble strength
giving the premium of the light.

            – Hildegard von Bingen, *O Ignis Spiritus*

RESTORATION DAY: SEPTEMBER 22

I address myself to you because you are my friend, my servant and the prelate of my Albigensian Church. I am exiled from the Pleroma, and it is I whom Valentinus named Sophia-Achamôth. It is I whom Simon Magus called Helene-Ennoia; for I am the Eternal Androgyne. Jesus is the Word of God; I am the Thought of God. One day I shall remount to my Father, but I require aid in this; it requires the supplication of my Brother Jesus to intercede for me. Only the Infinite is able to redeem the Infinite, and only God is able to redeem God. Listen well: The One has brought forth One, then One. And the Three are but One: the Father, the Word and the Thought. Establish my Gnostic Church. The Demiurge will be powerless against it. Receive the Paraclete.

> – The Revelation of +Jules Doinel
> (Valentinus II) , 1889

ST. MICHAEL THE ARCHANGEL: SEPTEMBER 29

Lighting a red candle:

> In the name of Light increasing, we summon
> Michael, the Defender, Lord of Fire and Prince of
> the Legions of Heaven. May he guard this Chamber
> and give due witness to the acts here taken. Come,
> mighty Michael, and grace us with thy presence.

ST. FRANCIS: OCTOBER 4

> Above all the grace and the gifts that Christ gives to
> his beloved is that of overcoming self.
> – St. Francis of Assisi

HOLY TEMPLARS: OCTOBER 13

Friday the Thirteenth of October, 1307: Acting in the name of the Pope, the brutal agents of Philippe IV le Bel of France arrested, tortured and later executed nearly all the Knights of the Order of the Temple in France. Philippe's motives were avarice and jealousy of the Order's temporal power, but he was aided and sanctioned in this totalitarian savagery by Rome on the pretext that the Templars were universally embracing heresy. Later however a cowed Clement V pardoned the Templars of any wrongdoing, but the murders had been committed, the Order broken, and the surviving members cast to the furthest borders of Christendom.

In kingdoms defiant of Rome, particularly Scotland and Portugal, the Order continued for decades if not centuries. In other regions, it merely changed its name or clothed itself in the trappings of other Orders, such as the Knights Hospitaller. But the two centuries of Templar corporate might and unchecked wealth had come to an end.

The Knights Templar were for the most part homicidal thugs, for the lesser part obedient, orthodox Catholics, and for the least part Initiates of Johannite (John the Baptist) Gnosticism. Despite the hylic nature of Order (obtaining, occupying, owning and killing things) it also served secretly as a repository for Gnostic Wisdom, with the Grand Masters ensuring the continuity of Johannite Tradition and thought. However rough the cup, it bore the wine that is the blood of the Logos. The Templars stand as icons of chivalry, nobility, sacrifice, honour, and service.

Under torture, some Knights confessed to the adoration of an icon of a severed head – remeniscent of the head of John the Baptist – known as "Baphomet", and encoded name for Sophia, Goddess of Wisdom.

Item, that in each province they had idols, namely heads.

Item, that they adored these idols.

Item, that they said that the head could save them.

Item, that it could make riches.

Item, that it could make the trees flower.

Item, that it made the land germinate.

Item, that they surrounded or touched each head of the aforesaid idol with small cords, which they wore around themselves next to the shirt or the flesh.

> – Inquisition charges against the Templars,
> August 12th 1308

Given the very strong associations with Johannite Tradition within the Order, it seems most likely to me that the sacred relic most prized by the Templars was, or was believed to have been, the mummified head of John the Baptist. That the Templars repudiated the crucifixion and denied the divinity of Jesus is well documented. This is exactly what we should expect if the Templars' ruling echelon believed that John and not Jesus was the Christ: an affirmation which would still result in them calling themselves "Christians".

The word "Grail" is derived from the word for a shallow serving dish, really more of a tray. The countless depictions of the severed head of John the Baptist traditionally show the head placed in just such a dish – which would certainly bear "the blood of Christ" by the understanding of the Johannites.

The lesson is that no measure of secular power that we can possess – military, financial, political – can withstand the onslaught of Archonic forces should they choose to exert themselves, regardless of either our innocence or ignorance on one hand or our spiritual gifts on the other. There is no physical castle we can erect against greed, against totalitarian megalomania. Only with *gnosis*, with Wisdom, with compassion, can we erect the citadel of the heart.

The weeks between today and All Hallow's Eve is known as Umbers, and it marks a period of reflection and detachment from the outer world, a time of turning inward to fortify the heart's chapel and its battlements. It is an invitation to visualize the private Sanctuary of heart's Wisdom – a space of stone and candles and stained glass, it smells of oak and dust and leather and sandalwood.

> So now the Holy Thing is here again
> Among us, fast thou too and pray
> That so perchance the vision may be seen
> By thee and those, and all the world be healed.

May all those suffering find peace and dissolution in the Pleroma.

God alone is enough.
Let nothing upset you,
let nothing startle you.
All things pass;
God does not change.
Patience wins
all it seeks.
Whoever has God
lacks nothing:
God alone is enough

    - St Teresa Avila

HALLOWS: OCTOBER 31

This is my favourite time of year here: the veil is so thin
Faerie flickers in the corner of vision, one finds pennies in
peculiar places, things go a little sideways and all that is
concrete gives playful way to the amorphous and abstract.
Everything – trees, cars, junk mail – is transubstantiated,
its root relocated from the materia to the mythic realm.
As Gnostics we're good at exploring this interstitial space.
The masquerade that the mythic wears in the mundane is
somehow just a little less convincing. Borders, boundaries,
prose transmuted into poetry. And so to the Dead, the
crossers of the border, those who are transported into
memory; we remember and pray for you, our spells bolt you
to our skin, if only for a little while.

> Blessings be on the Dead that are; Blessings be on
> the Dead that know. We remember those unmet
> and yet not unloved.

> May you return safely to that infinite shore at
> night's ending, and find peace in the dissolution of
> the Pleroma.

ST. THOMAS: DECEMBER 21

> If you bring forth what is within you, what you
> bring forth will save you. If you do not bring forth
> what is within you, what is within will destroy you.
> – *Gospel of Thomas, L70*

ST. RAPHAEL THE ARCHANGEL: DECEMBER 22

Lighting a yellow candle:

> In the name of Light arising, do we summon Ra-
> phael, the Healer, guardian of Air and Wind and
> Tempest, to guard this Chamber and witness the
> acts here taken. Come mighty Raphael, and grace
> us with thy presence.

NATIVITY: DECEMBER 25

Peace and Joy.

How impossible a wish, for our vain, short-tempered, belligerent species. How unimaginable, that within the rough manger of the created world, lies sleeping the infant spark of the Divine.

And yet the timeless recognition that this is so. Our birthright, the Divine seed sleeping beneath the snow of illusion, awaiting the spring and our own waking. How life gives magic to simple carbon, ribbons of living intelligence in our blood dancing, transforming us in an eternal, joyous miracle; the miracle of Incarnation.

Merry Christmas.

ST. JOHN THE BELOVED: DECEMBER 27

In the beginning was the Logos, and the Logos was with God, and the Logos was God. He was with God in the beginning. Through him all things were made; without him nothing was made that has been made. In him was life, and that life was the light of men. The light shines in the darkness, but the darkness has not understood it.

– *The Gospel of John*

Holy art Thou, that art, the Universal Fullness
Holy art Thou, that art, the self-perfecting Will
Holy art Thou, that art, who wills to be known and
is known
Holy art Thou, that art, the self-making Word
Holy art Thou, that art, more powerful than all
power
Holy art Thou, that art, transcending all
Holy art Thou, that art, better than all praise
Accept our mind's offering pure from soul and
heart stretched up to Thee,
O Thou Unspeakable and Unnutterable whose
Name is in Silence.

> *– Poimandres*

V. A GNOSTIC CONVERSATION

Why so "churchy" for a bunch of heretics? Are solitary
Gnostics a liability to a Gnostic Church? Why do you look
like Catholics?

Gnostic literature can be read as inspirational poetry.
Reflecting on that, incorporating that meaningfully, and
putting that into practice; none of this requires a Church.
But I think there is value in community, in liturgy, in
honouring collectively the passage of the liturgical year
and the sacramental cycles of your life; birth, adulthood,
marriage, death, acknowledging your mistakes and
nourishing the mythic self. So the Gnostic Churches enable
people to celebrate these cycles in a Gnostic context. There's
no agenda or exclusivity at all, and there's no "liability" in
those who find comfort and meaning outside the Church in
a more monastic setting, even if that's on the bus or in your
living room. We need to learn from each other's journey,
and that's harder to do if we view those who respond to
community or those who respond to solitude as a "liability".

It's vitally important to remember that the experience of
gnosis can happen within – and without – any religious
structure at all.

Now, Gnosticism as a religious path does not promise
to grant you enlightenment, but it creates a safe space
to celebrate and honour these flashes once they occur.
Gnosis in and of itself doesn't have anything to do with
institutionalism. That doesn't mean that an institution can't
grow and develop in order to serve those whose gnosis has
led them to contribute and participate. To boil water, you
put it in a pot. To cross the deep waters, you get in a boat.
That's all a Church is.

Now, the way of churching we use has two sources: one is
the pre-Christian religious structure of pagan Rome that

Christianity inherited and modified, the other is through the more-but-not-exclusively-secular civil service of the empire. The vestments we use come from those same traditions; four thousand years ago priests were wearing albs (white linen robes) to perform sacraments with bread and wine, and a thousand years ago secular lawyers and bankers and landowners wore chasubles. Modern business suits are evolved from military uniforms, but we don't read too much into that.

There is (and I believe was) also a deeper understanding of the pre-Christian nature of such things as the Offices, calendar, and indeed of the Eucharist itself. The Mass is the greatest and most accessible repository of the rituals of the Western Mystery Tradition, reminding us that Divinity is real and present - here/now, not there/then. The roles of deacon, priest, and bishop are echoes of Roman state religion, while the elements of the Mass have roots in Mithraism and the the cults of Dionysus. Such things are the cultural heritage, if not the property, of the western world.

So really, the only reason we "look like Catholics" is because Catholicism deliberately chose to look like that which preceded it. Catholic priests wear the zuchetto, which is exactly the same as the Jewish yarmulke and serves the same function.

Setting all that aside, as a Gnostic priest I wear the collar as a shorthand. People get that I'm sworn to a lifetime of service, listening, advocacy, and cheerleading your spiritual journey. You can tell me something in confidence, or turn to me for help. You have to admit that's pretty handy – a great deal is communicated in a very short period of time.

You present a very different model of Gnosticism than the academic definitions. Are you suggesting the scholars are wrong?

The usual academic definition usually includes something like this: Radical dualism and rejection of the world; considering the flesh as evil; anti-semitism in the form of the demonization of the Jewish God; elitism and pre-destination of the saved; a Christian heresy originating in the second century CE.

The problem is of course that the Gnostic texts don't support that definition. This is a late second century charicature of Gnostic ideas put out by orthodox "heresiologists" or heresy-hunters. Some of these unfounded charges are even embraced by a minority of pro-Gnostic contemporary writings, like the Clark Emery list, which includes an acceptance of the anti-Jehova position. I think it's fair to challenge this position as superficial.

The thing is, some of the Gnostic texts are entirely non-Christian, some are pre-Christian, others are supportive of Judaism, and some speak quite lovingly of the created world. The evidence doesn't fit the theory. So scholars like the University of Washington's Michael Williams want to erase the term Gnosticism altogether and call us "biblical demiurgicals", which is misleading because the majority of Gnostic texts don't even mention the Demiurge. Other academics such as Bart Ehrman disagree with disposing of "Gnosticism", arguing we're better off knowing what we're talking about rather than introducing new, cryptic terminology.

I think the biggest difference between the prevailing academic approach and the modern Gnostics is that Gnostics are looking at the texts themselves and seeing what they have to say, rather than trying to impose any specific agenda upon them or trying to make them fit with what early Christian propagandists said about them. The four themes outlined in the beginning of this book came out of a vigorous textual analysis of the Nag Hammadi scriptures. This is what they actually say: Gnosis matters. Everything flows out of God. The spark of God is everywhere and in everything. And there are mysteries to celebrate life and love and season.

This thematic approach – looking at Gnostic material as a literary genre as distinct as detective fiction or epic poetry – seems thus far to be the only way to make sense of the sometimes contradictory writings we find in the Sethian/Valentinian/Thomasine/Johannite/Middle Platonist continuum. Admittedly, a degree of placing all these different schools in a Gnostic continuum is aesthetic. Gnostic bishop and author Dr. Stephan Hoeller has said that identifying Gnosticism is like having a musical ear; in this sense we can see all these different composers keep returning to the four central themes.

This is not to say that there's not some difficult material in there. These books were written by different people in different cultures, and some of their statements reflect these cultural values. For some of these people it was critical to understand the names and heirarchies of angels and so forth. You see this in Judaism and Islam and early Christianity too. But if you make a list of, oh, fifty things to talk about in scripture, you'll see that eighty percent of the Nag Hammadi writings focus on these four critical points; knowledge of the heart, aspects of one-ness, immediacy of the spirit, and the sacraments.

If Gnosticism can be understood as a literary genre as you said earlier, what is the aesthetic of Gnosticism?

Recently I was standing in front of a small bronze by Rodin, "Fallen Angel, 1895" It's extremely sensual but also tragic, two nude forms folding into one another; one Illusion, the other Earth. The piece is unapologetic, resigned, hungry. It conveys a sense of loss, but also of endurance, of virtue and nobility.

The Gnostic Restoration, occurring as it did in 1890's France, happened in the artistic context of the Symbolists, encompassing visual arts, typography, dance, and even early cinema, Like the pre-Raphaelites who inspired it and the Art Nouveau which evolved from it, art of this period is imaginative and romantic, fluid and mystical, resonant and sensual. Mucha, Mackintosh, Moreau. This certainly is evocative of the flavour of the salons of ancient Alexandria which gave birth to Gnosticism. It was shamelessly syncretic; a little from Persia, some Greek, pre-Jewish semitic myths, North African tribal religions. It was the voice of the collective unconscious of the entire Silk Road.

Why do others use this term "Gnosticism" to describe things so far outside the realm of these Hellenized Jews and their myths?

Gnosis is a pretty general term meaning intimate experiential knowledge as opposed to abstract, theoretical knowledge, so I think the word is pretty much "up for grabs". If you want to use it to describe any kind of enlightenment from any culture, I think it's appropriate or at least arguable.

Gnostic*ism*, on the other hand, is the specific pre-Christian syncretic movement of the later Hellenic world, fusing Judaism, Greek philosophy, and Alexandrian Hermeticism. A "Gnostic" is one who identifies with this culturally-specific movement. We can widen that circle a little to include individuals who expanded on the themes and aesthetic of that culture, but these are exceptional and extraordinary individuals like William Blake and St. Julian of Norwich and St. Francis. But really, that's as far as we can take the term and preserve any practical meaning.

Some, inappropriately I think, use the term "gnosticism" to describe any idea, movement, or expression even obliquely related to enlightenment or non-ordinary "peak experience"; this would make all Sufis, Quakers, Shamans, philosophers, Buddhists (and even some drug-users) "gnostic". This stretches the word so far that it includes almost everything, and then becomes meaningless. It can also be seen to diminish other traditions which are doing their own thing in their own right: A Tibetan monk is not a Gnostic anymore than a Sufi is a Tibetan monk.

Admittedly I don't see how we can prevent anyone – from UFO conspiracy buffs to television psychics and South American sex-cultists – from abusing the term. I think you can just educate people that there's this incredibly rich cultural legacy of myth and symbol out there that is challenging, authentic, and rewarding.

Now we have to balance this idea of owning the word Gnosticism with the real desire to keep moving forward, to extend and expand the frontiers of spiritual experience. We can't stand still and say "This wasn't in *The Gospel of Thomas* so let's ignore it". We have to honestly view the scriptural horizon we have and understand it as a tool, the product of a culture that was a response to a world very different from our own. The purpose of getting a workable, thematic definition of Gnosticism is not to end debate but to make sure that as we move forward we're starting out from the same place, with a consistent set of tools and language. Blake said "I must create a system or be enslaved by another man's. I will not reason and compare, my business is to create." Does that make Gnosticism hard to categorize? Absolutely. But we can acknowledge that without surrendering altogether.

What's the role and purpose of myth in Gnosticism?

I think it's important to remember that our culture didn't pop out of nowhere. We owe so much of how we organize our inner lives to the Greeks, and how we organize our outer lives to the Romans. In a very real sense, their stories are still our stories. January and March and Wednesday are named after pagan gods. We also can't deny the degree to which our culture is shaped by bible stories, from the Garden of Eden and Noah's Ark to the Wedding at Cana and Judas' kiss. We also keep returning the core of stories from Robin Hood, from the Grail quest; themes of identity and seeking and challenge.

So as Campbell and Eliade and others have illustrated, we are in a way carved out of a solid block of these stories. We are composed of them. Our lives our retellings of these myths. Understanding their themes and navigating their currents can offer valuable insights into who we are and where we're headed. To that end, we have to remember that the characters and settings of these stories are us; the angels and demons, the knights and the dragons are aspects of ourselves we need to make peace with before moving on. Identifying, confronting, and incorporating these archetypes is the work of the spiritually maturing adult.

The Gnostic myth deals with the fall of Wisdom and the origin of the world we live in. It serves to illustrates that most of the things we concern ourselves with – authority, prestige and regulation and clocks and money – are not part of the natural world but rather artificial systems that have been imposed upon the world by human failings; fear, jealousy, ignorance. We've set up these authorities as false gods. But there's a redemptive element to the Sophia myth which is about remembering and reconnecting, about unconditional love and the secret joy of getting away with something.

The main obstacle is literalism and the hunger for externalization. This process is difficult, so a quicker, more simplistic understanding can be very attractive at times. We can take a Jungian approach to the idea of Archons, for example, and understand them first as patterns of behaviour, then as complexes, then as "splinter psyches" which as a kind of egregore inform and influence culture as though they were third-party entities. Which they're not – they're ideas, and they can't exist independent from us even though it seems we're at their mercy. But we made them up. The only extent to which they are superpersonal is in their aspect as the dark heart of the collective unconsciousness. There's a tremendous danger in assuming that the Archons are real external malevolent entities out to control our thoughts. That's abandoning the gift of myth for paranoia. It takes a message of inheritance and responsibility and turns it in to one of powerlessness and abdication.

The myths of Gnosticism are valuable when we understand them as myths, as stories which are symbolic of human processes. They serve as maps to regions explored by others before us. But to externalize and concretize is to mistake the map for the territory, which is a very common and very human failing.

What is the process of incorporating these myths?

Well first there's a feeling of *aporia*, or "roadlessness". A feeling of disorientation and a sense that "this is not the deal". There's that certainty that something is wrong with the universe, and creeping paranoia that a) this is somehow not the real world and b) that the forces in charge of this world are hiding something secret, something powerful.

Then there is epiphany. The big light bulb over the head, the primal "Aha!" that reveals the glowing spark of divinity in all things. A perception of real and immediate and undeniable truth in art and life and joy and beauty and the sacred real.

Of course then there's the *agon*, the "struggle". This is where things get ugly. The problem is, there are opposing currents to your epiphany. There are ideas entrenched in the world which are very threatened by different ways of seeing. People start to say they're "worried about you". This is where most people either give up and deny their epiphany, or become hurt by the whole experience. The real struggle is in finding equilibrium – knowing what you know, and continuing to live in the world. Rendering unto Caesar. Sitting down with the Archons and negotiating some kind of truce.

107

Perseverance leads to *gnosis*, which is a kind of sustained and integral epiphany in this context. Maintaining that *gnosis* is *charis*, a state of grace. This is what all of this is for, to get to that place of abiding love. But it is a difficult road; Philip K. Dick said that to know the principles of Gnosticism is to court disaster.

Are Gnostics Christian?

Although Gnosticism is distinct from Christianity, Gnostics are unwilling to surrender our connection to it, just as we are unwilling to give up our inclusion of Plato or the Wisdom literature of Judaism and the Hermetic material. Admittedly the Gnostic interpretation of Christianity is very different from modern mainstream Protestantism, but so too is modern Protestantism a radical departure from, say, the Coptic Church or any other surviving voice of the early Church. The Gnostic approach to Christianity can be accurately described as *esoteric*, from a Greek idea meaning "deeper" or "further in."

Now we have to understand how messy and contradictory early Christianity was, and how varied it was, borrowing ideas from the world around it. The borders were extremely untidy. Gnosticism, as a crossroads religion, already had this kind of syncretism built into its DNA, so incorporating Christian imagery and character was a perfectly natural evolution in its self-expression. Gnosticism, being an identifiable thematic movement before Nicea, is definitely closer to how the classical world understood "the Jesus movement" than what most people understand Christianity to be today. This doesn't mean to say that Gnosticism is the true or original Christianity, just that Gnosticism kept the context of its origins in a different way that Christianity chose to.

Am I a Christian? I Know that I am redeemed by the fallen word, the Holy Logos whose incarnation, sacrifice and resurrection are evidence of divine love in the world. This is an elemental aspect of what shapes my view of the world as it unfolds for me . My internalization of this story is similar to millions, if not tens of millions, of people who identify themselves as Christian. I have chosen to honour the indwelling Logos, and to give that intelligence the deciding vote in how I live my life. But I personally do not identify as Christian, although most Gnostics do. Because of the tradition of Sophia, there are many pagans and even Jews who identify as Gnostic as well.

Did the early Christian Church really get rid of Gnosticism?

The first person to refer to himself as Gnostic was St. Clement of Alexandria (150 - 216 CE), who embraced Greek philosophy in a Christian context and argued that one shouldn't abandon *gnosis* in the acceptance of faith. He remains a saint in the Roman Catholic Church today.

The common story to rank-and-file Christians – not to biblical scholars or even clergy, mind you – is that Jesus passed a very clear message to the Apostles who accurately understood it and accurately conveyed it to their communities, who accurately recorded it and so on. This presents the idea of a consistent, monolithic orthodoxy which later encountered the heresy of Gnosticism and rejected it. But that early orthodoxy is a complete fiction – it didn't even begin to gel until well into the fourth century, and interpretations were extremely localized even through the Middle Ages. This works both ways: orthodoxy couldn't reject Gnosticism because orthodoxy didn't exist yet, and likewise the charges that ancient Gnostic texts are somehow anti-orthodoxy is likewise misleading. The Nag Hammadi Library can't refute monolithic orthodoxy for the same reasons it can't refute the steam engine.

The early church argued for centuries about absolutely everything, and versions of scripture each community had varied widely, with contradictions more prevalent than agreement. Gnosticism became just one part of that dialogue. That chaos left a great deal of room for

some deeply spiritual people to explore and expand on
Gnostic themes within the Catholic Church. Some were
exterminated as heretics, others were hailed as Saints. In
the case of Joan of Arc it was both. Paul himself, sometimes
called the first Christian, touched on a number of core
Gnostic ideas in his writings often using specifically Gnostic
terminology.

Even today there are very deep currents of Gnosticism
within Eastern Orthodoxy and Roman Catholicism. The
ancient meditative practice of hesychasm, widely accepted
in the Eastern church, seems very Gnostic to me.

Do Gnostics deny the historical Jesus?

It's helpful to remember that when Gnosticism first
intersected Christianity, the emphasis was on what we later
call a "high Christology", on the divinity of Christ rather
than the daily events or even teachings of the Jesus stories.
Certainly the current trend is to humanize the historical
Jesus, and this is the work of authors like John Shelby Spong
and the Jesus Seminar. Others challenge the evidence for
doing so. Certainly nobody wrote about a Jesus movement
during the events themselves. But we have to remember
absence of evidence is not evidence of absence. Regardless,
these stories don't need to be historically true to be valuable,
both personally and with regards to understanding those
who authored them and those who responded to them.

Personally I don't find this demythicized, un-Christed Jesus
to be all that compelling. I don't think you can make Yeshua
stand on his own without the Christ archetype. By removing
the myth of the Incarnation from the man, we come out
relatively empty-handed. By pretending Christianity sprang
ex nihilo from the Judean scrub is to drain the lifeblood out

the Western Religion. By pretending that Christ isn't also Osiris-Dionysus, isn't Bacchus and Orpheus and Attis, by removing Jesus from all these rich stories is to commit the Christian heresy of Arianism, for which its original proponent was punched in the nose by Santa Claus in 325.

There's an interesting Greek idea buried in the two words for life: *bios* and *zoe*. *Bios* is the individual life, your biography, an instance or specific example of a bigger idea. That greater theme is *zoe*, like zoology, a story writ in entire species. This is very telling about the nature of myth, which many people misunderstand. The common take is that there's an event, something happens, and the story grows in the telling. "There really was a King Arthur, a Lancelot, a Camelot, and the details just got layered on and confused over time". But of course myth doesn't work this way at all. We don't start out with the *bios* of a wandering Rabbi and end up later with the *zoe* of a world-changing Christ. It's just never that convenient, and it's misleading to assume the "reality behind the legend" mechanism. It works the opposite way: we fold *bios* back into *zoe* to make actual events easier to understand.

We carry in each of us an archetypal story, a well of imagery and narrative, which whirls and eddies around historical events and people. Once energized by myth, entire groups of people, even cities, become distilled into characters in fables – but the myth always predates whatever half-understood history to which the legend becomes, eventually, attributed. Even St. Augustine recognized that Christianity was older than Christianity, in this way.

Can we rely on the Gnostic Gospels when they come so much later on than the Canonical Gospels?

The current scholarship sees the canonical Gospels of Matthew, Mark, Luke, and John all being written down early in the second century, based on oral traditions we first hear about in 110 CE. The oldest Gospel we have actual proof of is *John* from about 130, and Dr. Elaine Pagels suggests that the writers of the last half of that were familiar with the Gnostic *Gospel of Thomas*. Iranaeus, who decided that there should only be four Gospels, was familiar in 190 with the Gnostic Gospels of Philip and John and Mary and Judas and *The Gospel of Truth*. So all the Gospels, Christian and Gnostic, were written down roughly in the same era in the early middle of the second century. Obviously all of these are coming from older verbal sources, but archaeologically we have to see them as contemporaries.

112

Why the recent attention to the Gnostic Gospel of Judas?

Well, we only just found that, so there's been a lot of discussion. I think the text doesn't stand on its own; it needs to be seen in context of the *Gospel of Mary* and the *Secret Book of John*. These are what we call "frame stories"; they use characters familiar to the audience, usually with a "pay attention" message, then they introduce some fairly dense and difficult philosophical material, then return to the character narrative. In no way can these be seen to be history. We don't pretend that Jesus said this or that Judas said that. These are parables, employing well know folk characters. But we argue that you need to see *Matthew* or *Luke* in the same way.

Does modern Gnosticism require a new theology of the body?

The most common misunderstanding of Gnosticism is that we somehow reject the physical body and the sensual world. I think you have on one hand the erotic imagery of Jewish Wisdom literature from which Gnosticism drew the Sophia myth, Valentinus' use of erotic symbolism as a metaphor for spiritual union, and the fact that Gnostics were ordaining female bishops. On the other hand we see the Christian desert fathers literally running away from the touch of women, condemning marriage as prostitution, embracing celibacy and condemning procreation. Compare that to the bridal chamber analogy, so recurrent in Gnosticism, which is so deliciously earthy. So we're coming at a theology of the body from two very different directions.

Now, in Christianity we see the idea of bodily resurrection at the end of days. When the world ends, thousands of years after you're dead, ta da! you have the brown eyes you were born with (if you were born with brown eyes). You have a set gender and height and hair colour. This is a remnant of Egyptian theology where the body-soul is immortal and retains its form forever. In this theology, which Christianity inherited via Judaism, your soul, your you-ness, begins when you are given a body, and your essence is a collaboration between body and spirit.

Gnosticism has a more abstract view of physical incarnation and is much closer to Buddhism. The flesh isn't evil, but it's not perfect. You can learn a lot from it, but it will let you down eventually in its season just like a dying flower dropping petals. That's just the way it is. You don't get those petals back. So Gnosticism looks beyond this problem and says the essence of the flower isn't defined by petals dropped but by something else, something deeper. Our bodies are not ourselves. And how could they be? We are fragments of the Fullness that was old before the concept of time. We pre-exist our bodies. So we're no more identified by them than we are by a pomegranate we enjoyed yesterday. This is a very liberating theology for the disabled, the transgendered; it seems more fair somehow.

What is a modern Gnostic service like?

It's quiet, and seems very traditional on the surface, with candles and an altar and readings. Clergy with specific roles from lighting candles to blessings and offering communion. The understanding of all these things however is quite different from what you might be used to. The candles represent alchemical elements, as do the archangels. Prayers are to Word and Wisdom, as male and female aspects of the Infinite. There's music and poetry and the sign of peace, all that good churchy stuff, but usually these are employed as deliberate tools to stimulate parts of the psyche and nourish the imagination. It's less about worship of a "something out there" than an affirmation of our commitment to be present and mindful. There are many layers, but there's nothing scandalous and it's something you can bring your grandmother to. Almost all Gnostic churches have an open eucharist, which means you can show up and receive communion without subscribing to one specific point of view or other. This is left to individual preference and conscience.

Is Sophia the Goddess?

I use the word Goddess as a shorthand, but really no. She's a myth, a symbol for an aspect of something greater than the symbol can express. Looking back to Egyptian religion, where we see the term *netjeru* or "names", the various personalities we see as Isis, Osiris, Horus (Aset, Wesir, Heru) etc. are really taken to be aspects of one infinite reality, and the symbols are there for the practical purpose of simplification. Like many facets of one gem. We see the same thing in a Christian church, where there's an infant, a teacher, a crucified man, a lamb, a dove, and a vine – all there to represent different aspects of one idea of Divinity. The aesthetic of Sophia is very attractive to those traditionally inspired by the Divine Feminine: Women, artists, writers, poets, witches. In both Greek and Hebrew the word for spirit is feminine, and Gnosticism has always identified the Holy Spirit with Wisdom Herself.

How does the Holy Grail factor into modern Gnosticism?

I think the Grail stands as a kind of mythic code for the inheritance of Gnosticism in what's been called the Western Mystery Tradition. It's an archetype that resurfaces constantly in Western storytelling; the cauldron of Cerridwen, the platter bearing the head of John the Baptist, the cup of the last supper, the cup of blood from the crucifixion, and in current interpretation the womb of the Magdalene. Predominantly it represents the object of the quest, the hero's journey: It is that for which we are all ultimately seeking. The philosopher's stone. *Gnosis.*

It's an apt metaphor and fits well into the aesthetic of the mediaeval troubadors - who are inextricably entwined with the Cathars - and the later French mythographers who romanticized the Cathars into a kind of Gnostic ideal. For modern Gnostics, the myths and their lessons *are* the Grail, and the intoxicating wine it bears is *gnosis* itself.

118

VI. MODERN GNOSTIC CHURCHES

The Apostolic Johannite Church is a Gnostic Christian communion, continuing the church founded by French Freemasons in 1804. With three international bishops, the AJC operates several parishes throughout the United States, Canada, Mexico, Australia, and Spain. The AJC runs a formation program for Gnostic clergy, St. Raphael the Archangel Theological Seminary, headquartered in Calgary, Alberta.

> "We affirm that there is one Great, Unknowable, and Ineffable Godhead that made manifest the Universe through Emanation and that while the Universe is contained within this Divine Godhead, the Godhead transcends it.

> We affirm that every Being contains the 'Sacred Flame,' a Spark of the Divine and that Awareness of the Sacred Flame within constitutes the highest level of Self-Knowledge and the Experience of God simultaneously. This act of Awareness, which is held to be liberating, transcendent and experiential, is called *Gnosis*.

> We affirm that there are many ways in which Gnosis may be experienced. Thus, we promote freedom of thought in pursuit of one's inward Path towards the Divine, whether that pursuit is modern or ancient in origin, or individual or communal in experience."

The Ecclesia Gnostica is perhaps the best-known Gnostic Christian church, due to its leadership by author Bishop Stephen Hoeller. Based in Los Angeles it has smaller missions in Seattle, Portland, Salt Lake, and Oslo, Norway. Its website hosts an excellent collection of homilies for the liturgical year written by Rev. Steven Marshall.

> The Ecclesia Gnostica exists for the purpose of upholding the Gnostic tradition and to administer the holy sacraments to those of God's people who are attracted to the altars of the Gnosis. An active ministry of parish work is thus an essential feature of this church. The Los Angeles parish of the Ecclesia Gnostica holds eleven regularly scheduled church services and four catechetical lectures each month in order to serve the spiritual needs of its congregation. The Regionary Bishop presides over the majority of these activities.

The Ecclesia Gnostica Mysteriorum just relocated after 30 years from a storefront church in Palo Alto into a freestanding church building in Mountain View. Lead by Bishop Rosamonde Miller, the EGM has a strong emphasis on the Sophianic tradition and the legacy of Mary Magdalene.

> We acknowledge and celebrate ritual—so deeply ingrained within our own primitive natures. Since primitive times and against all rationality we continue to search for the Unknown and Unknowable within and beyond perceived reality, the Great Mystery beyond birth and death. The rituals that we celebrate in our Sanctuary, with their flow of poetry, music and rich metaphor often lead us

beyond ordinary reality. When consciously celebrating their mystery, a paean of joy often bursts from our souls that connects us to the root and totality of our beings—as well as with that which has been, is, and is yet to come.

We are not dualists and do not follow any one school of Gnostic "thought," ancient or modern, such as Valentinian, Basilidian or Marcionite, among others. We today, as did our early Gnostic ancestors, maintain our freedom to inquire and explore all levels of existence, unfettered by the consensus beliefs of our society and times. We do not follow "Gnostic doctrines," the term amounting to an oxymoron, any more than any other belief handed down through the centuries. Gnosis is a matter of experience, not belief.

The Gnostic Church of Mary Magdalene is active in Portland and Seattle.

> We exist as a Church to refresh the ideal of one-world spiritual community, across all boundaries implied or imposed by the limited cultures of time and space. We give ourselves to our role model and Patroness Mary Magdalen. She is our Saint and Mother, both in her person and in her service as Apostle of Apostles. Her life holds for us a link to the eternal Wisdom of Genesis, manifested on Earth to support our Master, in flesh as in spirit. We understand the Sacred Marrage by witnessing her relationship with Master Jesus, and because of this we elevate her as the Holy Mother of our Church.

Our Mission: The Gnostic Church of St. Mary Magdalen exists for people of every background and faith whose soul longings are directed towards finding a balance between the Divine Feminine and Masculine in Christianity.

The Order of Saint Esclarmonde is a Gnostic, monastic lay Order open to women and men, sponsored by both the Gnostic Church of Mary Magdalene and the Apostolic Johannite Church. Novices are not required to be members of either church.

The purpose of the Order is to provide structure to committed, solitary, traditional spiritual practice. Nuns and Monks of the Order commit to mindfulness, daily contemplation, and community action through charitable works. During daily prayer, nuns and monks wear the traditional white alb and white cincture as both a reminder of their connection to others undertaking this work, and as a symbol of purification.

Saint Esclarmonde was an early 13th century Cathar mystic. She is traditionally identified as the woman who successfully debated the virtues of Catharism against the founder of the Inquisition, St. Dominic. Legend has it that when the Inquisition finally came to take her to her execution, she turned into a dove and flew away. Her legend was romanticized during the Napoleonic era to the point where she became a kind of Cathar Joan of Arc and patroness of the revival of art and mysticism of the 19th century.

FURTHER READING

While the academic study of Gnosticism can be both dense and daunting, several popular books aimed at non-academic audiences are easily available:

The Gnostic Bible
by Willis Barnstone and Marvin Meyer

Sophia: Goddess of Wisdom, Bride of God
by Caitlin Matthews

The Many Paths of the Independent Sacramental Movement
by John P. Plummer

Promethea (a graphic novel in five volumes)
by Alan Moore

The Gnostic Gospels
by Elaine Pagels

124

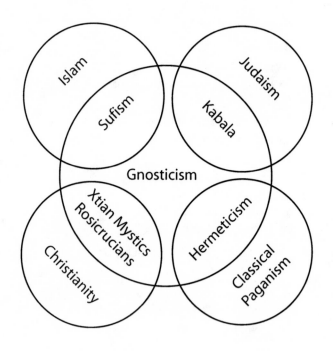

Islam

Judaism

Sufism

Kabala

Gnosticism

Xtian Mystics
Rosicrucians

Hermeticism

Christianity

Classical
Paganism

AFTERWORD:
A RELIGION FOR AIRPORTS

There's a man outside Starbucks right now, holding up half a sheet of plywood with REPENT on one side and LAKE OF FIRE on the other. Half a sheet of plywood is not a light placard, yet the man is dancing; filthy, eyes rolling, beaming, ecstatic. Passers-by stop and take photographs with their cell phones.

Up the block attractive women in their 30s in Lulu Lemon yoga gear and $200 Nikes are toting red "Tradition" Starbucks cups up the stairs to a studio of blonde hardwood, incense, and soothing musing flowing out of Bang & Olufsen speakers. They will bend their bodies into ancient forms, breathe, and fold forward until their ponytails sweep their pastel-toned neoprene matts.

Early Christian texts mirror this collision of paths in spiritual practice. The Apostles, speaking in tongues and walking barefoot out of the Jerusalem scrub, decry the literate, articulate, and classically educated Athenians.

This is not to say that the Jews were not logical and literate, nor that the Athenians were not ecstatically bathed in blood from sacrificial livestock: but a distinct emphasis of one culture on one flavour of experience and another culture on another flavour of experience was evident: The Temple vs. the University, ecstasy vs. theology.

The Athenians were well versed in metaphor, myth, poetry, speculation, abstraction; the recipients of the Pauline epistles were urged towards acceptance of the literal reality of demons, miracles, healing, prophecy. These are not necessarily exclusive, but the historic paradigm conflict made room for the archetypal conflict of the Dionysian vs. the Apollonian world views.

The Athenians bathed, read poetry, honoured their gods with sacrifices, and grew olives in nice, tidy rows: they must have perceived the Christians as barking from dumpsters with a radically unsophisticated message of superstition and anti-intellectualism. Once the Christians took hold it was the worst of the mob that characterized the movement: the murder of writers and teachers, the burning of libraries. In two generations Christian Rome dismantled "civilization" as it had been known for a millennium – the plumbing stopped working, medicine all but disappeared, infant mortality soared while literacy plummeted, ushering in what we now call "The Dark Ages" but known to Christians as "The Age of Faith".

We need to understand that many on both sides of this cultural divide had *gnosis*: that the Alexandrian Jews who were the first Gnostics were familiar with both the transcendent, irrational and primal experiences of Orphic and Isis cults as they were with the rational critiques of Greek philosophy. The primary theme of early Gnostic and Hermetic texts is about the reconciliation of archetypes: as above, so below.

What "saved" civilization were those communities which integrated classical values with Christian values; those who found balance between radical spiritual practice (albeit in the monastic atmosphere of silence and contemplation rather than Dionysian orgies) and the pursuit and preservation of classical education. While the Empire dismantled itself in spasms of corruption and holy wars (people were no longer slaughtered in the name of the Emperor but in the name of Christ), remote communities of dedicated individuals preserved the DNA of civilization in the amber of Irish monasteries. This was only possible because of the balance sought, the reconciliation of Dionysis and Apollo, of Jerusalem and Athens.

Fast forward to the Enlightenment, and modernism, it the re-visioning of the religious experience. The gatekeepers of theology have been, for the last century or so, eminently reasonable. Cautious about literalism, suspicious about demons and miracles. Flexible. Rational. Modernist. Athenian.

The majority of the world's Christians do not share this Northern theology; they come from African, Asian and South American cultures in which demons and miracles are factual realities and psychology, ecumenism, and inclusiveness are seen as Satanic devices. The barefoot glossalalians are emerging from the desert once again. Only whereas in the second century, these cultures met one another on a fairly equal footing, this time the North is vastly outnumbered.

127

What will Christianity look like once a wave of Southern New Jerusalem overtakes the Athenian North? How will inclusive, tolerant, ecumenical Christians react when faced with literally hundreds of millions of book-burning homophobes who insist that women be silent in Church?

What happens when a generation of hip, aware, tattooed, multilingual, educated, environmentally-responsible Episcopalian urbanites who stopped at one child (if any) is overcome by a majority of dozen-siblinged fundamentalists who think being gay is caused by demonic possession? The North has been outbred by the South, and the fundamentalists are basically just waiting for us - and our egalitarian, feminist, green, tolerant, "reasonable" Apollonian culture - to die out.

So what we will see is a greater degree of supernaturalism in the upper echelons of culture, just as it has always existed in the *hoi polloi*. The fundamentalists won't be burning libraries, but contrarian books will get even harder to publish. We'll also see a greater tolerance of other Dionysian approaches, such as Yoruba and Santeria. This is not necessarily a bad thing – it seems to me that the need for supernaturalism serves a purpose, and the fewer "monsters under the bed" have given us more serial killers out of some bizarre compensation. Certainly the romantics among us are not going to be put off by a statistical spike in the belief in Faeries.

So as Christianity gets noisier, messier, crazier – whither goest Gnosticism?

Creedal "just believe" religions aren't so good with such jarring paradigm shifts; they usually result in bloodshed on a large scale. But Gnosticism is the ultimate particle-or-wave religion; reconciling paradox is in our pneumatic DNA. We've always been able to switch modalities from rapturous vision to elaborate cosmological correspondences and back again before the first bottle is empty. This intellectual territory is messy, but for us it's home.

Gnosticism has always been a religion for airports: its thread has traced from Judaism to Christian mysticism, from Kabala through Sufism, from the Hermetic revival of the Renaissance to Gaian neo-Paganism. As the century hands us new challenges, we need to respond with deeper questions; in many cases questions with their origins in other cultures and other time periods.

To survive as an integral, coherent religion, mainstream Christianity is going to need to look to its monastic past. But it does seem to me that Gnosticism has something to offer - in the freeform jazz riffs of the theological beatniks that we are - to those wanting to walk a middle road: a road to neither Jerusalem nor Athens, but to Alexandria.

BIBLIOGRAPHY

Barnstone, William and Meyer, Marvin, *The Gnostic Bible*. Boston: Shambhala, 2003

Brown, Raymond E, *The Community of the Beloved Disciple*. New York: Paulist Press, 1979

Churton, Tobias, *The Gnostics*. London: George Weidenfeld and Nicolson, 1987

Doresse, Jean, *The Secret Books of the Egyptian Gnostics*. Rochester: Inner Traditions, 1986

Freke, Timothy and Gandy, Peter, *Jesus and the Lost Goddess*. New York: Crown, 2001

Goodspeed, Edgar J. (Ed.), *The Apocrypha*. New York: Vintage, 1989

Hoeller, Stephen A, *The Gnostic Jung and the Seven Sermons to the Dead*. Wheaton, Ill: Quest, 1982

Hoeller, Stephen A, *Jung and the Lost Gospels*. Wheaton, Ill: Quest, 1989

Küng, Hans, *The Catholic Church: A Short History*. New York: Random House, 2003

LaCarriere, Jacques, *The Gnostics*. San Francisco: City Lights, 1991

Lane Fox, Robin, *Pagans and Christians*. New York: Knopf, 1986

Matthews, Caitlin, *Sophia: Goddess of Wisdom*. Wheaton, Ill: Quest, 2001

Pagels, Elaine, *Beyond Belief*. New York: Random House, 2003

Pagels, Elaine, *The Gnostic Gospels*. New York: Random House, 1979

Pétrement, Simone, *A Separate God*. San Francisco: Harper, 1984

Plummer, John, *The Many Paths of the Independent Sacramental Movement*. Berkeley: Apocryphile, 2005

Robinson, James M. (Ed.), *The Nag Hamadi Library*. New York: Harper and Row, 1988

Rudolph, Kurt, Gnosis: *The Nature and History of Gnosticism*. New York: Harper and Row, 1987

Scott, Walter, *Hermetica*. Boston: Shambhala, 1993

Segal, Robert A (Ed.), *The Allure of Gnosticism*. Peru, Ill: Open Court, 1995

Singer, June, *A Gnostic Book of Hours*. New York: Harper Collins, 1992

Smoley, Richard, *Forbidden Faith*. New York: Harper Collins, 2006

I know you're out there. I can feel you now. I know that you're afraid. You're afraid of us. You're afraid of change. I don't know the future. I didn't come here to tell you how this is going to end. I came here to tell you how it's going to begin.

131

– The Matrix

Printed in the United States
117397LV00005B/4/A